PSYCH ONLINE

Patricia M. Wallace
University of Maryland—University College

 **McGraw-Hill College**

Boston   Burr Ridge, IL   Dubuque, IA   Madison, WI   New York   San Franciso   St. Louis
Bangkok   Bogotá   Caracas   Lisbon   London   Madrid
Mexico City   Milan   New Delhi   Seoul   Sydney   Taipei   Toronto

McGraw-Hill College
*A Division of The **McGraw-Hill** Companies*

PSYCH ONLINE, SECOND EDITION

 This book is printed on recycled, acid-free paper containing 10% postconsumer waste.

6 7 8 9 0 CUS/CUS 0 3 2 1

ISBN 0–07–232023-0

Editorial director: *Jane E. Vaicunas*
Senior sponsoring editor: *Joseph Terry*
Editorial assistant: *Fred Speers*
Senior marketing manager: *James Rozsa*
Project manager: *Jill R. Peter*
Production supervisor: *Deborah Donner*
Coordinator of freelance design: *Michelle D. Whitaker*
Typeface: *10/12 Century Schoolbook and Univers*
Printer: *Quebecor Printing Book Group/Dubuque, IA*

Freelance cover designer: *Jamie O'Neal*
Cover image: © *Sergio Spada/Graphistock*

Library of Congress Catalog Card Number: 98–89207

www.mhhe.com

Table of Contents

6 ABNORMAL, CLINICAL, AND COUNSELING PSYCHOLOGY.....108

List of Boxes

Traffic Jams on the Internet   13
Is the information superhighway becoming a parking lot?

Search Engines on the World Wide Web   20
Learn how to find what you need on the Web.

Your Electronic Persona   21
Online, they don't know if you have two heads.

Netiquette Guidelines for Online Discussion Groups   23
Learn the rules of etiquette to avoid embarrassing gaffes.

APA Journals Go Online   27
Some of the most important psychology journals are now available on the Web.

Citation Styles for Electronic Media   40
How do you cite material you find online in your research paper?

Experiments in Perception: Evolution of a Software Program   43
Keeping software up-to-date is no easy task.

Interactive Tutorials on the Web   49
Rapidly advancing Web technology supports many kinds of interactivity.

Putting the Web to Work for Undergraduates: Psych Web   53
One of the first psychology-related sites on the Web just keeps growing . . . and growing.

TIPS and the TIPSTERS   55
Stop in and listen at the psychology faculty lounge.

Social Decision-Making and Prisoner's Dilemma Simulations   71
Computers do a great job at mathematical games, and these games are used to study the dynamics of social decision making.

The World of the Paranormal   80
If you like "The X-Files," you'll love these resources.

1 Introducing Psych Online

For students of psychology, and that includes all of us involved in this wide-ranging field, working with online and computer-based resources has evolved into bursting file cabinets and a low-tech mound of scribbled notes. Unlike the journal literature, which is nicely organized and electronically searchable in databases, or the psychology-related books – also easily located with library catalogs – the enormous volume of online and computer-based material is 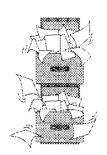 more difficult to probe. Cataloging systems are still primitive, if they exist at all. Although keyword searches are possible for some of the material, the searches often turn up a bewildering volume of sites with or without titles. Information about important resources is often passed around by word of mouth or its electronic equivalent. Though the medium is faster, the process itself is not that different from what our ancestors did centuries ago before organizing and cataloging systems were standardized.

These resources are rapidly becoming the most important ones for psychology students, faculty, researchers, and practitioners. To get your arms around what is out there, to find the resources you need without endless hours of surfing and experimentation, and to have some context to evaluate new resources, you need a guidebook. *Psych Online* is a compendium of online and computer-based resources to help you understand the scope of these immensely useful materials and decide which ones you want to explore.

What Will *Psych Online* Do for You?

Provide Quick Tips and Tools

Psych Online includes a brief overview of the most important categories of resources and tips on how to use them. Instructions are kept to a minimum. This book is not an introduction to the Internet or a manual on using your computer. You can get this kind of information in many other places if you need it.

Provide a Psychology-Oriented Context

Psych Online isn't an alphabetical list of every resource out there, nor is that the goal. With new resources emerging daily and older ones (or even brand new ones) disappearing into the ether, a comprehensive list would be impossible and not even desirable. Instead, the goal of *Psych Online* is to highlight a large range of resources, point out which ones are extremely useful, and place them all into a context appropriate for the discipline of psychology – one that emphasizes the interests of people searching for resources rather than the type of resource. For example, if you're involved with social psychology as a student, faculty member, or researcher, you're interested in resources of any kind that relate to your field. It won't matter if you can get to them via the Web, an e-mail to the author, an automated subscription to a mailing list, or an anonymous ftp, just as it doesn't matter if written material is obtained from a journal or textbook. With *Psych Online*, you can form a large framework for the kinds of resources available in several goal-oriented categories and when new ones come to your attention you have a context in which to evaluate them.

See the Big Picture

Though you may be a veteran on the use of some of these resources, you may not be aware of the big picture. Most people's knowledge of what is out there is spotty and uneven because so much information is distributed informally. You might, for example, hear about a great mailing list through the grapevine, join it, and then spend many hours reading all the e-mail. But you might not learn about many other discussion forums on similar subjects, one of which might suit your needs far better.

Save Time

Those of you who surf the Net, join discussion forums, or download software know that these resources can be a time-sink of gargantuan proportions. For example, exploring the World Wide Web with a modem is great fun – for a while – but every graphics-filled page can take an irritatingly long time to download. You can't just browse the Web the way you can browse a bookshelf. You can't thumb through a Web site the way you can thumb through a book to see if it meets your needs. We are now well past the stage at which we can afford to just wander around, delighting if we find something interesting. The electronic tools are becoming more familiar so we don't need to dwell on computer-related details, as fascinating as these may be. We need to get some work done.

Lead You to a Variety of Resources in Psychology

The resources in this guidebook come from many different sources and fall into several categories. Many are Web sites with special relevance to psychology. A large number of entries describe software products from companies, universities, or individuals who will share their work with their colleagues. The range of software runs the gamut from the multimedia CD-ROMs to older DOS and Macintosh programs that still run well on modern computers and still contribute something useful to the pool of resources, despite their less flashy interfaces. Some important entries describe the major computer-based and online library resources for psychology, which have grown considerably since the first *Psych Online* was published in 1997. A great many mailing lists and newsgroups are listed as well, and people involved in psychology have made much use of the online discussion to hold debates, share ideas, and keep in touch. *Psych Online* includes information on how you can access or obtain everything listed.

Explore Resources from Anywhere in the World

The online world makes it possible to communicate with people all over the planet and learn what is happening in psychology in many different countries. It also enables us to draw from a global pool of resources. With e-mail, you can contact a faculty member or student on the other side of the planet as easily as one across the campus to learn more about the software they're developing. On the Web, of course, you sometimes don't even know the geographic location of the site; the constraint of distance on our ability to take advantage of psychology-related resources has, for all practical purposes, vanished.

Learn About the People Who Develop Computer-Based and Online Resources

In the traditional world of publishing, becoming an author is an arduous process. However, almost anyone can develop Web sites, shareware, and discussion groups and offer them to the entire world, virtually overnight. It's a very democratic environment, and psychology students have been especially creative players. *Psych Online* includes interviews with some of the people who have contributed to this high-tech arena.

Reflect on the Psychology of the Electronically Mediated World

This frontier is a treasure-trove of material for innovative psychological research. The social psychology of electronic discussion forums, for example, is a fascinating subject in its own right. *Psych Online* highlights some of the ways human behavior is changing because of the new media, and some of the resources listed deal directly with the topic.

Identify the Gaps

Computer-based and online resources in psychology are spotty in coverage. Some areas have far more material than others, and this guide will help you see where the gaps are. If you are developing resources yourself, you'll be able to see where you can make a contribution.

The Organization of *Psych Online*

Organizing the resources in *Psych Online* is not an easy or straightforward task, given their range and the breadth that so many of them show. A Web site with pointers to hundreds of other locations and a variety of discussion forums can be very hard to categorize, particularly when it is evolving rapidly and adding new resources all the time. A discussion group can change its focus quickly, depending on who is participating. A purely subject-oriented organization based on the subspecialties of psychology would not work well.

Instead, *Psych Online* adopts a goal-oriented organization, one that is more suited to the needs of the people in this field. This approach recognizes that students, faculty, researchers, practitioners, and people in need of support have overlapping but somewhat different goals when they are searching for resources. Although two discussion groups might deal with addictions, for example, one may have a research-oriented focus and the other may be a recovery support group. Content and even membership might overlap, since addicts are interested in the research and students and researchers are interested in the personal experiences of addicts. However, the orientations of the two groups highlight different goals of the participants. Instead of grouping these together under a single subject heading, I put them in separate sections. Librarians are debating how to organize and categorize material of this kind, but this approach should help you understand the orientation of the resources as well as their subject matter.

The book begins with quick tips on how to use the many resources in the book, but the general assumption is that many of you already know how to use most of them and just need a few reminders, procedures, and definitions. In any case, this kind of information is available through many other sources, particularly the manuals that accompany your computer and software.

The second chapter includes a glossary for reference, and it covers the icons used in this book to identify the type of resource. These will help you recognize at a glance whether the resource is a Web site, a gopher site, a software program, a lively or sleepy discussion group, a resource loaded with text material, or any of a number of other categories. A special symbol, the POL-STAR, is used to draw your attention to very valuable resources that will be useful to the whole psychological community.

Chapter 3 covers the megasites in psychology, including the giant databases and library resources. Chapter 4 lists the resources that are primarily for students and faculty, particularly at the introductory level. Chapter 5 explores more specialized resources within psychology, and these are grouped by discipline. Many of these resources are also for teaching and learning, especially in more advanced classes dealing with neuroscience, sensation and perception, cognition, social psychology, or other academic areas.

Chapter 6 lists resources in abnormal psychology, clinical psychology, counseling, and other areas related to mental health. People in practice or students leaning toward this area in psychology will want to explore these extensive resources directed toward researchers, students, teachers, practitioners, and people who are suffering from various behavioral disorders and need support. The chapter also includes a number of self-help resources.

The previous edition of *Psych Online* included a final chapter on the proprietary services, such as American Online and Prodigy, whose special content is accessible only to account holders. Some have some specialized material pertinent to *Psych Online*, but, since so many more psychology-related resources are now openly available on the Internet, this chapter was omitted for the current edition.

A Word About Shifting Sands

Anyone familiar with some of the resources in this book knows that the rate at which materials come and go is alarming. Quite a few that were listed in the first edition of *Psych Online* have been dropped because they are no longer available. Valuable resources you stumble upon after an agonizingly slow search and many dead ends may disappear or move to a different host just after you enthusiastically inform all your classmates or colleagues about them. There is no parallel to this in the arena of the printed word or the commercially produced video. This guidebook is not quite the same as a list of suggested readings or a catalog of psychology-related videos. Those list-makers can be reasonably certain that the resource will still be there a year or two from now, even if the book goes out of print or the video is no longer available commercially.

The reasons for the volatility are many and varied. A shareware author may decide not to share the software any longer, or the program may have been developed for an obsolete computer platform or programming environment. A student-Webmaster may head to graduate school after erasing the files in the directory. Mailing lists and newsgroups evolve and change over time, and many become extinct. A formerly very lively asynchronous discussion may just die out from lack of participation, even though a review may show that many people are still subscribed to it. A surprise post to a long-dead discussion group often triggers remarks such as, "Wow, I didn't even know I was still on this list."

Lists of resources available on the Internet can, in principle, be easily updated to reflect such changes. But this kind of checking and rechecking takes considerable work, and many online lists and catalogs contain references to resources that simply don't exist any longer, or that are so old their creators would be shocked to hear from an interested party. For the first edition of *Psych Online*, I sent out hundreds of snail mail and electronic queries to people and organizations all over the world about psychology-related resources I'd seen online, and the number that were returned with "address unknown" was astonishing. One software author, Barney Beins of Ithaca College, replied with amusement that I was the first person in several years to inquire about his programs and that either the programs were extinct or he must be. For this second edition, researcher Caroline McKeldin and I rechecked every entry and were not very surprised to see how many disappeared from the map.

Despite the volatility of many electronic resources, some stability is emerging. Although a Web site created by a student for a class may disappear tomorrow, sites such as PsychNet and Coombsweb will not. The environment will continue to be a world of shifting sands, but the megasites and super-resources will be here for some time because they fill our need for important psychology-related materials. Just as the printed version of *Psychological Abstracts* evolved into the electronically searchable *PsycINFO*, the most important computer-based and online psychology-related resources will continue to grow and adapt as computer platforms change, greater bandwidths become available, and the capabilities of our electronic tools increase.

Several Words of Thanks

For this edition, I especially want to thank Caroline McKeldin, who worked tirelessly as a researcher on this project, contacting all the sources and adding her own brand of warmth and wit to many entries and boxes. She is a psychology graduate and author of the humorously eccentric books called *Japanese Jive* and *New York Smells*. (The latter is a scratch and sniff collection of postcards that feature unique aromas from the Big Apple.)

We both owe a great deal of thanks to the hundreds of people who responded to queries with information about the resources they had to offer. Many of those who replied are not commercial software developers or professional Webmasters. They are students, faculty, and others involved in psychology who have something useful to share, often at their own expense. When you contact any of the people listed in this book, please recognize that many of them may be offering a particular service or resource to the psychological community on a collegial basis. Most mailing list owners, for example, are not paid extra for their hard work, and they appreciate your patience when technical problems arise that they can't solve immediately. Many software developers write programs to use in their own classes but are pleased to share their work with others who might find it useful. They may not be able to provide much technical support, and they may ask for a small payment to cover expenses or a shareware fee.

To the hundreds of people from all over the world who responded to our queries and sent packets of information, demo disks, CD-ROMs, instructions, and words of advice, many, many thanks – not just from me, but on behalf of the people who read *Psych Online* who may contact you to learn more about the exciting work you're doing to add innovative, high-tech resources to the world of psychology. Keep up the excellent work.

2 Tips and Tools

To take advantage of the resources in this book and feel comfortable when new ones come to your attention, you need a workstation with certain features; some software and software skills; and access to cyberspace, specifically, the Internet and World Wide Web.

This chapter is not intended to make you an instant UNIX guru, a telecom technician, or an Internet trainer. You're probably more interested in psychology than you are in the details of file transfers and terminal emulation, anyway. Fortunately, people need far less expertise in computer science now than they did in the early days of the Internet or microcomputers. The technology is maturing, but it still isn't quite as simple as pressing the PLAY button on your VCR. This chapter provides the essential information, an overview of the tools you'll be using, and a review of the common jargon. If you are already a high-tech wizard, hanging ten on your Web surfboard, go on to the next chapter.

The Workstation

The resources in *Psych Online* require a workstation equipped with a microcomputer, a printer, and several software packages. You will also need a connection to the rest of the world, either through a modem and a telephone line, or a direct connection. And, finally, you'll need a host computer account with your college or university, an Internet Service Provider (ISP), or some proprietary online service that provides its own content as well as access to the Internet.

The microcomputer is the brain and heart of your workstation, and the features it includes determine, to a large extent, what you will be able to do. The most important components are the processor, the disk drive, the memory, and the monitor.

The central processing unit (CPU) is the actual brain of the computer and determines how fast it can process information. The two most important features to notice about the CPU is the type of processor, such as the Pentium or Pentium II processor used in Intel machines, and the clock speed of the processor. For example, a Pentium might be offered in a number of versions with different clock speeds, measured in megahertz. In a computer ad, usually the very first description for the model will identify the level of the processor and its clock speed. For example, "333-Pentium II" indicates the type of processor and that the machine runs at 333 MHz; an older, used model described as 486-66 indicates a 486 processor (forerunner of the Pentium) running at 66 MHz. These two features contribute substantially to the increasing cost of the computer at different levels.

RAM

The amount of random access memory (RAM) in a microcomputer is an extremely important variable in its overall performance, though many people pay little attention to this component when they purchase a new computer. RAM functions like short-term memory or working storage. For example, when you start working on a very long word-processed document, the amount of RAM will determine how much of that document you can access immediately and how much must remain on the disk in permanent storage. While human short- term storage is usually measured in "chunks," the capacity of RAM is measured in megabytes (MB, millions of bytes) and is usually expandable. One byte represents eight bits of information and holds the code for a single typewritten character such as an A, a comma, or a hyphen. A computer with 8 MB of RAM, for example, could hold the equivalent of about eight million characters of information, though much of it is needed for information other than your actual document.

Modern software requires considerable RAM to operate, particularly if you are trying to use more than one software package at the same time. The message "Insufficient memory" is a frequent sight on modern computers, meaning that the user will have to close some applications to make more RAM available.

Earlier models of computers measured their RAM in kilobytes, or 1000s of bytes. For example, the 286s usually came equipped with 640 KB of RAM. Today, a computer with 4 MB of RAM is considered very low-end. For the last edition, I recommended at least 16MB, but now 32 to 64MB is very common, and much needed to run modern software at a reasonable pace. Though prices have dropped, memory is still not inexpensive, and it is one of those options many people forego because they can't see its value in the store. Human short-term memory, at least according to the classic experiments by Miller, is limited to 7 chunks, plus or minus 2. Fortunately, if you find you don't have enough working storage in your computer you can usually add it later. (Too bad we can't add RAM to the brain.)

Hard Disk Drive

The most important permanent storage area for information is the hard disk drive, whose capacity is also measured in megabytes or gigabytes (GB, trillions of bytes). The first hard drives for  microcomputers held from 10 to 20 MB of information. This seems pitifully small by today's standards -- already into the gigabyte range. The lesson here is that the need for hard drive space grows much faster than you expect. Modern software, also known as "bloatware," will rapidly gobble up your hard drive space. Although you can conserve disk space by storing infrequently used programs and data on floppy diskettes or tapes or by using software that compresses your data into smaller files, you will find that your hard disk fills up surprisingly quickly. If you are buying a computer now, you should consider at least 4 GB of hard disk storage. If you will be downloading large data sets, videoclips, or sound files, you will need far more. A short videoclip could occupy many millions of bytes.

Floppy Drive

Floppy drives for microcomputers come in two main sizes: 5 1/4 inch and 3 1/2 inch. The drives accommodate diskettes of different sizes. The 3 1/2 inch floppy drive has become standard on all computers now, but, because many people have data stored on the larger 5 1/4 inch diskettes, manufacturers generally provide the ability to add that drive to the system. The 5¼-inch diskette holds about 1.2 MB of data, while the 3½-inch diskette holds 1.44 MB. Because backups are so important, and the floppies don't hold much data even when you compress it with a backup utility, many people add a device to their workstation that supports removable hard drives (zip drives). With this, you can back up critical data onto hard disk cartridges that hold far more data than a floppy. Another backup option is to add a tape drive to your system.

Monitor

The monitor is the display device that you will be viewing for hours. Many manufacturers attempt to keep their prices low by including poorer-quality monitors with their systems, so it is wise to actually "test drive" a system, with the actual monitor it comes with,

before buying. You might save some money if you buy a monochrome monitor, but you won't be happy with it. Virtually all modern computer monitors are color and vary in size from about 15 inches (diagonal) to 21 inches. If you like to keep three or four applications open at the same time, you should consider a larger monitor.

CD-ROM/DVD-ROM Drives and Multimedia

The CD-ROM drive enables the computer to access data stored on CD-ROM platters, which hold about 650 MB of information. This is equivalent to about 450 3½-inch diskettes. Almost all CD-ROM drives sold with microcomputers are read-only, and you can't save any of your own information to the shiny platters the way you can on your hard drive or floppy diskettes. For example, if you want to download a videoclip from the World Wide Web, you can't save it to your CD-ROM disk. The file will probably be too big for a floppy disk, so you'll have to save it to your hard drive, thus eating up more of your most precious storage compartment. People who really love to save these large files may want to buy a special type of recordable CD-ROM drive that allows them to write data to blank platters, and then use them in regular CD-ROM drives.

The ability to concentrate so much information in an inexpensive format has made it possible to store videos, sound files, huge amounts of text, and other byte-hungry applications and make them available to the microcomputer. Without the CD-ROM, it would not be feasible to create and market large data sets or multimedia applications at reasonable prices. Even very brief videos and audio files take up huge amounts of storage space, and the amount of data needed for many bibliographic applications is also too massive to distribute on floppies.

Emerging now is the DVD-ROM, a newer technology that will supplant the CD-ROM because it enables the platters to hold 4.7 GB of data -- quite an improvement over the current 650 MB. The second generation of these drives (DVD-2) can read all the older CDs, including the ones that are created with CD recorders, and audio CDs.   The vast amount of storage space on these platters will allow developers to embed multimedia elements, interactive games, gargantuan databases, and even full-length movies.

In addition to the CD-ROM and the DVD-ROM drive, a multimedia microcomputer requires a sound system and speakers. These come standard on Macintosh computers and are widely available on IBM-compatible systems. The speakers that come with multimedia computers are often poorer quality, though sufficient for most applications. If you don't mind the less than perfect sound quality, you can play your audio CDs on your computer and listen to music while you work. However, an audio CD player can't read the platters used in computers.

The Software

The software industry is trying to convince us that we should buy more and more packages and upgrade constantly to add functionality that will enable us to do things we never planned on doing anyway. This approach helps the hardware industry because bloatware requires more hard disk space, more memory, faster processors, and higher-resolution monitors.

For the psychology-related resources in this book, you will not need expensive software. You will need to be able to use some of the most common software packages, some of which are free. The following are the most important software tools and skills you'll need.

Graphical Web Browser

You will need browser software such as Netscape Navigator or Internet Explorer to access the Web sites in this book. Current versions of these programs are widely available through a multitude of sources, including online, for free. Keep in mind that these programs have grown quite large, so a download via modem could take many hours. A very useful feature of browser software is the ability to save the address of a Web site you are visiting, while you are visiting it. These are called bookmarks in Navigator and favorites in Explorer, and they can be organized according to topic. The next time you wish to visit that site, you can go directly to your list rather than conduct a tedious search with keywords.

Word Processor

Most people consider the word processor to be the single most useful piece of software they own. These programs are so loaded with features that the user's guide can be hundreds of pages long. You probably never use most of these features, but, for the purposes of this book, you may need to know something about how to use your word processor to handle files in ASCII (pronounced ASK-ee) format. This is particularly true if you will be dealing with downloaded statistical files.

Save and retrieve commands of a word processor ordinarily handle binary files stored in the format your word processor can decipher, complete with hidden codes for boldface, subscripts, and other formatting features. These files can usually be read by other word processors if they have the right conversion utility, but you will run into occasions when you need to read, save, or otherwise manipulate a "plain vanilla" version of a document.

The plain vanilla version of a word-processed file is called ASCII, and your word processor will have a means of saving and retrieving text in this standard coding format. In Microsoft Word, for example, the ASCII version is called a "text file." If you want to view a data file that you downloaded from the Internet, you should retrieve it in its plain vanilla version rather than allowing your software to convert it, and you should also save it again that way.

File Management Skills

You will need to know how to move around and examine the files on your computer's disk drives, create directories, remove them, and run programs. Many software programs in *Psych Online* are not commercial products with slick installation routines and user-friendly manuals, but their psychology content could be just what you need. To take advantage of these resources, particularly if you are accustomed to being insulated from the computer's operating system by Macintosh or Windows and you've only installed commercial products that handle all the details, you will need to learn the basics of file management. Higher-order file management skills are particularly important to keep your hard drive organized and to avoid chaos in computing when you are exploring shareware, freeware, or demos. If you don't plan ahead, you'll wind up cluttering your hard drive with hundreds of files you're afraid to delete because you can't remember what they do.

E-mail Software

To join mailing lists and communicate with your friends and colleagues via the Internet, you will need e-mail software. Some e-mail software is integrated with the browser (e.g., Netscape Mail), while others are standalone products.

An especially valuable feature of most e-mail software is the ability to automatically filter incoming mail. If you join an especially active mailing list, for example, you may want to set your software to automatically file mail from that list to a special folder so it doesn't clutter your inbox. Then, when you have time, you can go to the folder and read several days' worth of discussion.

A number of companies are offering free Web-based e-mail accounts as a way to bring visitors to their Web sites. The advertisers who display ads on those sites are paying for these services. Examples include AltaVista from Digital (http://altavista.digital.com) and Microsoft's Hotmail service (http://www.hotmail.com). One advantage to these services is the ability to check your mail from any workstation on campus that has Web access without having to configure any specialized e-mail software.

Virus Protection Software

Downloading software from the Internet, from bulletin boards, or from online services makes you vulnerable to viruses. Before running any software you obtain from such sources, you should scan it for viruses. You should be particularly careful about this and include it in your automatic routine when you start your computer each day if you're lazy about backing up your files.

Decompression Software

Freeware and shareware available for downloading from online sources are often compressed so that they consume less storage space and can be transmitted across telecommunications lines more quickly. Once you have the compressed file on your hard disk, however, you will need to decompress it before it will work. If the software is relatively new, you may only have to click on the file you just downloaded, and the installation program will automatically do all the work for you. However, some resources in this book were created before those installation routines were widely available, so you may need to know how to decompress the file.

Most Intel-based microcomputer software can be decompressed with a program called pkunzip.exe. Macintosh users typically use a program called Stuffit to decompress. Pkunzip.exe can be downloaded from many sites for free. On the Web, do a search for pkunzip.exe and you will find the closest downloading sites. If you already have an older version of pkunzip.exe, download the newest version if you have difficulty unzipping any software.

Connecting to the World

To connect your workstation to other computers down the street or around the world, you will need a modem and telephone line or a direct connection of some kind.

The modem, which you will probably be using from your home, converts the analog signals carried by the telephone lines to the digital signals required by the computer when you are receiving information. When you are sending, the modem does the digital to analog conversion. When a phone number is dialed, your computer's modem starts a handshaking process with a modem at the host computer to negotiate the connection and begin exchanging information. Universities often have banks of modems accessible through the same number so, when you call the university, your call will be directed to the next available modem. A modem can be installed as an internal device in the microcomputer, or it could be an external device connected to the microcomputer with a cable.

One of the most important features of the connection you make to other computers is the speed of the connection, which is measured in bits per second (bp/s) and which is dependent on your modem's capabilities

(and those of the modem you call), not the speed or power of your computer. Modem speeds have increased in jumps over the years as data compression techniques have improved. Many modems in use today support 33.6 kb/s (kilobits per second) or higher, and, if you are buying a new one, I recommend the 56 kb/s variety, since you will be spending much time online. You may sometimes hear the words "baud rate" to refer to modem speeds, but this measurement scheme is correctly applied only to the slower, earlier modems, though you may still see it used in older communications software when you try to configure the parameters for a connection. If you have a 56 kbp/s modem but are connecting to a host with modem banks that support only 33.6 kbp/s, your modem will "step down" to the slower speed. Although you will usually want to establish the fastest connection you can, there may be times when you want to force the modem to use a slower speed by configuring your communications software. When the telephone line connection is noisy (or "dirty"), slower speeds may actually work better.

Increasingly, more and more options to connect from your home are becoming available. For example, the cable companies are implementing Internet services in some locations so you can connect using the coax cable they installed in your home for your television, rather than over the telephone lines.

Another option for higher speed connectivity is ISDN (Integrated Services Digital Network), offered in most locations through the telephone companies. You will need an ISDN adapter for your computer, ISDN service from your carrier, and an ISDN account with your Internet Service Provider. The ISDN service allows you to connect at maximum speeds of 128 kb/s.

Larger organizations, such as your college or university, usually have direct connections to the Internet that provide access to all the computers on campus via high-speed dedicated leased lines.

The Internet Host

When you connect to a host computer that is linked to the Internet, you start your session with that host and use many of its features, such as its e-mail services. The host will have an address that is a sequence of numbers separated by dots, such as 137.34.122.21, and it will almost always have a unique domain name linked to that numbering address that is (somewhat) more memorable, such as mugwump.c1.msu.edu or nic.funet.fi. Systems managers create all kinds of ways to make the Internet easier to use, and often a single host has multiple domain names, all of which refer to the same host.

Usually the domain name will tell you something about the host, such as its location or its general category. Domain names read from left to right, going from the most specific part to the most general. The rightmost portion is the top-level domain, which might be edu (educational institutions), gov (government agencies), com (commercial firms), net (computer networks), org (noncommercial organizations), mil (U.S. military), int (international organizations), or some initials to indicate the country. Examples of the latter are ca (Canada), au (Australia), uk (United Kingdom), se (Sweden), jp (Japan), in (India), and fi (Finland). You may notice a certain U.S. bias here. Internet addresses for U.S. hosts do not usually have us as the top-level domain but use the org, edu, or com designator instead.

Universities, companies, and other organizations often try to use their initials or full name as the second-level domain (such as apa.org, msu.edu, microsoft.com, or whitehouse.gov) so they are easier to remember. As the Internet adds more and more hosts, it is much harder for new institutions to obtain exactly the second-level domain name they want and still be unique.

Internet Service Providers

When you access the Internet, you go through an Internet Service Provider (ISP) that is paying for a high-speed connection to the Internet itself that can support many simultaneous users. The ISP provides you with a number of services that may include an e-mail account, telephone access numbers, software, installation and setup instructions, technical support, a unique address for your computer, a place to create your own Web pages, and others. Your university or organization will act as your ISP if you access the Internet from a computer connected to the network on the campus or at work. Your campus, for example, might pay an annual fee for a high-speed connection to an ISP that supports Internet access from computers in the labs, in the dorms, and on the faculty's desktops. Some universities and organizations also maintain modem banks so you can dial in from home through their Internet hosts.

If you want to access the Web from home and your university or organization doesn't provide the service, you can purchase it from one of the hundreds of ISPs throughout the world. ISPs advertise widely in local newspapers and on radio, and many are sending their information through direct mail. Celestin Company, Inc. maintains a large directory of ISPs at http://celestin.com/pocia/ with descriptions of the services and pricing plans.

Navigating the Internet

Once connected to the Internet, you can use your host (even if it is your own computer) as a home base and begin hopping around. Since the Internet is a vast, worldwide network of hosts and lines connecting them, all using the same

Traffic Jams on the Internet

The popularity and commercialization of the World Wide Web has created a very troubling situation for the Internet because the growth in usage is now geometric rather than linear. With the spectacular increase in the number of users, hosts, and transmission requests – particularly for the byte-hungry video and audio materials – traffic is a major concern. Some are pessimistic about the Internet's future and complain that it is basically unusable during much of the day.

You can help keep the Internet valuable by using it wisely. For example, before downloading a file you should check its size to be sure the file is worth the time and the Internet bandwidth it will consume. Don't make coffee while you wait 20 minutes for a download of the latest movie trailer from Paramount, which you might watch once and which will probably appear on TV, anyway. If valuable sites have a mirror closer to you, use them instead of creating transoceanic traffic. You can also set your browser so that it does not automatically retrieve graphics, and turn that feature on only when you need the pictures. Admittedly, the graphics can enhance your experience on the Web, but they are also bandwidth hogs.

Right now, many universities are offering full Internet access to students and faculty, and many service providers provide unlimited time for remarkably low, fixed monthly fees. However, some of the larger ones have already moved away from the unlimited plan and have begun adding hourly charges after the user hits a certain maximum (such as 150 hours of use) for the month. It may be only a matter of time before this kind of pricing structure is the norm. In any event, the Internet is a shared global resource, and it's something worth protecting.

---

protocol to negotiate transmission, you can hop about to any of the online Internet resources in this book, investigating the information available, searching databases, and downloading files to your own computer. Occasionally, you'll receive a message saying that the host you're trying to reach is down or is not responding, but you can always stop in at that site later to see if it is available.

Accessing Web Sites and Other Resources on the Internet

Psych Online uses the Uniform Resource Locator (URL) standard to identify and help you locate resources on the Internet, whether they are files, Web sites, gophers, or anything else. The first part of the URL indicates the type of object (Web site, file, gopher site, ftp site), and the two slashes precede the host computer name. The remainder of the URL indicates the directory locations on the host computer and the name of the file, if needed.

A URL for a Web site, for example, might be http://www.apa.org/

Entering this into your browser will take you to the default opening page for this address. The http stands for Hypertext Transport Protocol and this indicates that the object is a Web site. Other URLs might begin with gopher:// or ftp:// to identify other kinds of resources.

A URL for a more specific resource on a host computer, such as a specific file in a special directory, will have additional names after the host name. For example, the lengthy URL

http://cvs2.anu.edu.au/andy/beye/
beyehome.html

indicates the host name
(cvs2.anu.edu.au), which happens to be
in Australia (au); the directory (andy);
the subdirectory (beye); and finally the
name of the file in the subdirectory you
will want to open (beyehome.html). Even
though the URL may occasionally span
more than one line in printed text, you
should use no spaces when you type the
address. If you type in a URL correctly
and still receive an error message, you
might try "backing up" by omitting the
file name, or one or more of the
directories and subdirectories. For
example, you can see if the host exists by
entering

http://cvs2.anu.edu.au/

You can see if the andy subdirectory still
exists on the host by entering

http://cvs2.anu.edu.au/andy/

If you're lucky, the higher-level address
will have the correct links to the resource
you're trying to find. Systems managers
and Webmasters often rearrange their
directories and subdirectories, but the
main host address is usually more stable.
If you do find the correct site at a
different URL, you should make a note in
this book so you won't have to play Web
sleuth again.

If you still can't find the address,
it may have moved to a different host
entirely and left no "forwarding address."
This is not uncommon, particularly for
resources developed by individuals on
the hosts of commercial Internet Service
Providers. Perhaps they changed their
account to a new service and brought the
resource up there. It might also no
longer exist, or there may be a typo in
this book. (I hope not!) Try using one of
the search engines described in the box
in this chapter to see if you can track it
down.

The Web

A great many psychology
resources are available on the World
Wide Web, which is a rapidly growing
subset of resources on the Internet that
takes advantage of a special page-
description language called HTML for
Hypertext Markup Language. Web
browser software can interpret materials
prepared in HTML as special fonts,
graphics, page formats, and multimedia.
The Web has definitely changed the face
of the Internet and turned it, almost
overnight, into a far friendlier and more
beautiful place. Now, when most people
think of the Internet, they think of the
Web, not the text-based environment of
the past with all its arcane commands
and baffling procedures. Most of the
online resources in this book are,
fortunately, on the Web, so you will be
using your browser software to access
them.

Search tools to help you find sites
by keyword on the Web are many and
varied, and they include AltaVista, Lycos,
the WebCrawler, and others. (These are
described in the box on search engines.)
Many will return a list, sometimes a very
long list, that orders the hits according to
a measure of confidence with respect to
how well each hit matches your search
criteria. Although simple searches are
straightforward, you'll need to read the
instructions for each search tool to learn
how to use its syntax to access its
advanced features.

Gophers

In addition to the http://
designator for Web sites, this book
includes URLs for a very small number of
gopher sites (gopher://). The gophers are
menu-based systems running Gopher
software from the University of
Minnesota. Although they are now
nearly extinct as their content was moved
to the Web, a few still exist that contain
useful psychology-related information.
With a graphical Web browser, you can
usually enter the URL for a gopher in the

same way you do for a Web site. If you are using a text-based interface, the easiest way to get to a gopher site is to type the word gopher followed by a space, followed by the hostname for the site. This will "point" your gopher to the appropriate location. Gopher sites are usually open to anyone and no login or passwords are necessary.

FTP

Some URLs in this book begin with ftp://, which stands for file transfer protocol. These sites are often software repositories from which you can download shareware, demos, free programs, clip art, images, text material, and anything else that can be transmitted via the Internet. Again, if you're using a graphical Web browser, you can usually type the URL into the field and the software will do the rest. Ftp sites don't have the multimedia pizzazz that many Web sites do, but they are packed full of useful items for you to retrieve.

If you are not using a graphical Web browser, obtaining a file via ftp is a little more complicated. Most of the time, computer hosts that maintain material available through ftp support anonymous ftp, which means that anyone in the world can login to that site with the user name "anonymous," enter their own e-mail address as the password, and then retrieve whatever files interest them in the accessible directories.

The following session shows an example of how one would perform an anonymous ftp to another computer host to retrieve a file. The user Jane Doe has the userid jdoe, and her home computer is myhost.mycollege.edu. Jane wants to download a program file called goodfile.zip located in the pub directory at the ftp site called goodsite.gooduniv.edu. The file she wants to retrieve is a compressed program file (not an ASCII text file), so she must be careful to indicate this during her ftp session. She would only type the entries in boldface italics.

myhost > *ftp goodsite.gooduniv.edu*

Connected to goodsite.hostname.edu,
220-Welcome to the Goodsite
Home of the hottest
software repository on the planet
Name (goodsite) *anonymous*
331 - Guest login ok, send e-mail address as password
Password: *jdoe@myhost.mycollege.edu*
331 - Guest login ok, access restrictions apply
ftp > *cd pub*
200 PORT Command successful
ftp > *binary*
200 Type set to I
ftp > *get goodfile.zip*
200 PORT Command successful
150 Opening BINARY mode data connection for goodfile.zip (17064 bytes)
226 Transfer complete
Ftp > *quit*
221 Goodbye
Myhost >

The password you enter (your own e-mail address) will not appear on the screen as you type. Also, if you are retrieving an ASCII text file rather than a binary file, you will not need to set the session to binary.

Telnet

One more command you may need is telnet. This protocol enables you to hop from your own host to another and log in to it to run one of its programs or access its information. For example, you can reach the Conversational Hypertext Access Technology (CHAT) host in Canada, described in chapter 5, and run the CHAT program, by typing the following at your host's prompt:

telnet debra.dgbt.doc.ca 3000

In this case, the 3000 indicates the port on the other host you want to use, since it has been configured to run the program you are allowed to access. If you are using your Web browser, you can usually telnet to other hosts provided you have telnet software configured to work with your browser. In Netscape, for example, you will need to identify the telnet application you want to run under General Preferences, Apps, in the telnet box. There are many telnet software clients available for free if you want to access telnet from your browser. Once the telnet application is configured, you can type telnet:// in the field on your browser to launch the telnet software and then enter the details for the remote host to make a connection. Browsers vary, though, and some don't support telnet, so you will need to check the instructions on your own software.

Internet Mailing Lists

Participating in lively discussion groups is one of the main reasons you want to join the online world in the first place. For psychology, the mailing lists offer some of the most important resources. The breadth of activity in this arena is truly mind boggling and growing larger by the minute. With millions of people on the Internet and using online services, one can only imagine the range of topics that attract just a few, or thousands, of interested participants.

The Internet is home to several different kinds of discussion groups, and the commercial online services offer still more, each one vying for the online time and talent of people who have something to say or questions to pose. This section explains how to take advantage of the many psychology-related mailing lists available on the Internet. Be forewarned, though, that the popularity of mailing lists and forums waxes and wanes, and sometimes never gets off the ground. This guide includes an estimate of participation level as part of the icon. Even if you don't receive much mail, though, there may be quite a number of people subscribed to the list, so you might be able to bring it back to life with a probing query or discussion topic. The silent subscribers who read the mail but

rarely participate are sometimes called "lurkers," but the term isn't usually meant in a derogatory way.

A mailing list is a discussion group that relies on e-mail. You send e-mail to subscribe to it, send e-mail to a different address to post messages to the discussion group, and receive e-mail in your own e-mail box whenever anyone else posts a message to the discussion group. If you like getting lots of mail in your electronic mail box, the mailing list is the way to go.

If you've used distribution lists to send e-mail to a large number of people, you're already familiar with the manual version of the mailing list. The sender, or discussion group moderator, must enter each e-mail address manually and maintain the distribution list when changes, deletions, or additions are required. When discussion groups started growing into monsters with thousands of members, it became clear that a more automated solution was needed. Special software was developed that freed the moderator from the burdensome task of maintaining the mailing list and transferred much of that burden to the individual subscribers.

Mailing lists and other kinds of discussion forums can be moderated or unmoderated. In a moderated group, the moderator of the list may read every message before posting it to the group. He or she may choose to eliminate any inappropriate messages, especially ones that flame or insult other participants. In unmoderated groups, the participants can say whatever they want and no filtering is applied. There are also forums that fall between these two extremes, in which the moderator serves more as a facilitator – he or she doesn't filter any messages but keeps the discussion on track and warns any participants whose messages are inappropriate. Quite a number of psychology-related forums fall into this middle ground.

There are several software packages used to automatically manage the most popular psychology-related mailing lists. These are LISTSERV, Majordomo, and MAILBASE. These management systems run on a variety of host computers linked to the Internet. (Since LISTSERV software is so widespread in academia, you may hear people call a discussion group a "listserv.")

It is important to know what kind of software your discussion group is using, or at least understand a few of its most basic commands, because the commands to control your subscription to the group vary somewhat. A brief description of the most common commands for each of the systems follows.

For all mailing lists, you should send any commands that control aspects of your subscription to the mailing list software, NOT TO THE ADDRESS OF THE DISCUSSION GROUP. This error is so common that participants often receive daily messages from people who are trying to subscribe, unsubscribe, or perform some other function but are mistakenly sending their command to the group, which may include (literally) thousands of people. There may be technical problems at the server that interfere with the interpretation of commands, but, in this case, contact the manager of the group or host systems administrator privately. Don't send your complaint to the whole list.

LISTSERV

LISTSERV was originally created by EDUCOM as a basic "mail exploder," but its uses grew and its limitations became apparent. A revised version of the software developed at the Ecole Centrale de Paris in France added considerable functionality and efficiency to the original version. To subscribe to a LISTSERV mailing list, you send e-mail to an Internet address that begins with LISTSERV followed by the @ sign, followed by the host computer that hosts the group. For example, if you want to subscribe to INTROPSY, one of the mailing lists for psychology undergraduates, you would send an e-mail message to

LISTSERV@VM.TULSA.CC.OK.US

Leave the subject blank, but in the body of the message put a single line that reads

SUBSCRIBE INTROPSY Jackie Doe

You would substitute your own full name, of course. You are actually sending a message to an automated program that can decipher your message (as long as it is in the correct format) without human intervention. The program automatically subscribes you to the discussion group running on its host called intropsy.

Most LISTSERV software will reply to you with an automated notice of some kind, letting you know the status of your request. The message might tell you the list is nonexistent, or it might say the list is closed. If you're determined to join the group and you can't seem to subscribe automatically, you can sometimes contact the list manager via e-mail to describe your interest.

If your request was successful, the message would welcome you to the group and give you instructions on other commands you might want to send to the LISTSERV software that would help you control your subscription. The automated message will tell you how to get off the list, find out who else is participating in the list, or send a command to hide your own name from other people who might want to see a list of subscribers. You should save this automated message. If your e-mail program supports folders, you should create a folder for your discussion group and put this message into it so you can refer to it later. It will help you avoid some of the bothersome mistakes newbies make when they join mailing lists such as sending "unsubscribe" messages to the list itself, rather than the automated list server address. In addition to the automated subscription message, you may also receive a second automated message showing some statistics on CPU time or disk operations. This one is useless, and you can delete it.

Sometimes you will receive an automated request for a reply before you are subscribed. The managers of the list configured the software to do this because they want to be sure that subscribers actually exist and that their e-mail address is correct. If you receive a "command confirmation request" you will usually have to respond within 48 hours or your initial request will be ignored. To respond, you only have to reply to the automated message by typing "ok" in the body of the message and sending it off. You should not include a copy of the automated message in your reply. If you don't reply to confirm your subscription request, or you mess up the message, you'll have to start over.

The following are some common LISTSERV commands, though the LISTSERV software varies and managers configure it in different ways.

To subscribe:
SUBSCRIBE listname Yourname

To unsubscribe:
UNSUBSCRIBE listname

To temporarily stop receiving mail (such as over Christmas break):
SET listname NOMAIL

To turn the mail back on:
SET listname MAIL

To get messages in digest form (if available), rather than individually, and this is highly recommended for high-volume lists:
SET listname DIGEST

To receive a list of the names and e-mail addresses of other subscribers:
REVIEW listname

To receive information about LISTSERV commands:
HELP

Majordomo

Brent Chapman's Majordomo software also automates the mailing list process to facilitate discussion groups. For most Majordomo lists, you send commands to MAJORDOMO@HOSTNAME, rather than to LISTSERV@HOSTNAME. This is the tip off that the list is managed by Majordomo software, but a few sites keep people on their toes by using LISTSERV@HOSTNAME instead. Several mailing lists in this book, for example, are housed at LISTSERV@NETCOM.COM, which uses Majordomo, so, if you try to subscribe with "SUBSCRIBE listname yourname," your subscription request will be automatically rejected and you'll have to start over using Majordomo syntax and commands.

To subscribe to a Majordomo list:
SUBSCRIBE listname

To unsubscribe:
UNSUBSCRIBE listname

To find out who else is on the list:
WHO listname

To receive introductory info about the list:
INFO listname

To obtain a list of lists served by the server:
LISTS

You don't add your own name after the name of the list when you subscribe. If you do, Majordomo will usually send you a friendly rejection of your request with instructions on how to get it right.

Mailbase

Mailbase is an organization housed at Newcastle University in the United Kingdom that operates hundreds of mailing lists, some of which are psychology-related. You can obtain more information about its services at its Web site (http://www.mailbase.ac.uk/docs/).

Many of the lists are actually sublists with specialty discussions under a more general superlist. For example, CTI-PSYCHOLOGY is a sublist under the CTI-ALL superlist group. CTI-PSYCHOLOGY is a resource for educators looking for psychology-related software, and CTI-ALL covers a range of disciplines such as business, marketing, law, economics, and social work. Some Mailbase lists are closed to self-subscription, and you will need to contact the list owner to request entry.

The following are some basic Mailbase commands. You do not need to add the word STOP as the last line in your message unless you have configured your e-mail system to add something else at the bottom of your outgoing e-mails, such as a signature file. To make Mailbase more user-friendly, some of the commands have synonyms so LISTSERV users won't be too frustrated. For example, UNSUBSCRIBE usually works in place of LEAVE, to sign off a group.

To subscribe, send e-mail to
MAILBASE@MAILBASE.AC.UK
Put the following in the body of the message:
JOIN listname yourname
STOP

To obtain a Mailbase user guide:
SEND MAILBASE USER-GUIDE
STOP

To learn who is subscribed to the group:
REVIEW listname
STOP

To temporarily suspend mail from the list:
SUSPEND MAIL listname
STOP

To leave the list:
LEAVE listname
STOP

To obtain the names of archived files:
INDEX listname
STOP

Posting Messages to Mailing Lists

Now that you're subscribed to the mailing list of your choice, you will probably start receiving the messages other subscribers are posting, assuming the list is reasonably active. You'll probably join in the middle of some ongoing discussion, and many of the messages will actually be labeled "replies" to some message you didn't see. You should lurk for a while before jumping in to get the flavor of the conversation. When you're ready to contribute your two cents, you can send your message to the list address, which is usually the name of the list followed by the same host to which you sent your original subscription request. For example, you could send e-mail to

INTROPSY@VM.TULSA.CC.OK.US

to post a message to that group. You can also reply to other subscribers' postings.

The instructions in this book deal with the procedures for most of the major list manager programs, but you really need to save the instructions for each list you join. I've seen some with arcane commands, manually maintained by the list owners, that defy categorization. The diversity in list manager software commands and procedures is frustrating to mailing list participants who join many different groups. Perhaps in a few years some software giant will dominate the list manager software scene and we will have to remember only a few simple commands for all of them. However, this is mostly free or inexpensive software, so there is not much incentive. It seems the desire to communicate about academic subjects with colleagues around the world is outweighing the irritation of nonstandard interfaces.

Internet USENET Newsgroups

USENET News, also called Network News, Netnews, or just USENET, consists of discussion groups arranged in hierarchies according to type of discussion. There are literally thousands of active newsgroups sorted in top level categories such as:

comp (computer-related)
sci   (scientifically oriented)
rec   (recreation)
alt   (alternative)

Within each main category, there are newsgroups with increasingly focused discussion topics, such as sci.space.news, rec.arts.tv.soaps, and comp.os.ms-windows.misc.   Examples of psychology-related newsgroups described in this book include

sci.psychology.research
sci.med.psychobiology
alt.psychology.psychotherapy

By convention, discussion groups under the mainstream top-level hierarchies (such as comp, misc, news, rec, sci, soc, and talk) are established through a voting process of USENET subscribers, but anyone can start a group in the alternative (alt) hierarchy.

USENET is a more efficient means to establish discussion forums, compared with the mailing lists, because, instead of sending mail to each and every subscriber, USENET traffic is sent to the host computers as "newsfeeds." The messages posted can then be read by anyone accessing that host. This method results in less Internet traffic, though systems managers usually choose not to receive the feeds for some newsgroups for a variety of reasons. Some newsgroups may not be available at your site.

Search Engines on the World Wide Web

The total tally of Web sites is a moving target, but most agree that the Web has many millions of pages, with billions of words of text. Search engines are programs housed at Web sites themselves that allow users to enter one or more key words. The engine returns a list of sites that match (more or less) the user's search criteria. The engines maintain their Web directories by using automated "crawlers," "robots," and "spiders" that scour the Web continuously for new sites and name changes. Almost all the search engines offer their services to users for free. Many carry advertising to pay for their upkeep.

The search engines vary in capabilities and in the number of sites contained in their directories. Some, for example, support Boolean operators such as AND, OR, and NOT, and some include USENET groups and other resources on the Internet in addition to Web sites. Here are a few of the more popular search engines. Each has advantages and disadvantages, so you may want to try more than one for searches you are conducting.

AltaVista (http://altavista.digital.com/)

Excite (http://www.excite.com/)

Lycos (http://www.lycos.com/)

Yahoo! (http://www.yahoo.com/)

Increasingly, these sites and others like them are vying to become your "Web Portal," that is, the place you start your day on the Web. They offer a variety of services in addition to their search engines, such as free e-mail, news summaries, online chat, bulletin boards, free software downloads, disk space for your own Web page, and tips on Internet-based shopping. Yahoo's site, for example, includes access to a low-price finder tool with which you can compare prices of a particular item across vendors.

Although there are many psychology-related newsgroups, the level of conversation and quality of discussion vary considerably, and some of the unmoderated ones are loaded with flames, foul language, and brittle one-upsmanship games. The newsgroups are often more freewheeling, compared with the mailing lists. Partly because there are so many with similar titles, the newsgroups are heavily inundated with "cross-postings," meaning that a message is posted to many newsgroups at the same time. Although this happens on mailing lists, it is more common in the newsgroups and creates a fair amount of confusion.

Most of the search engines can be applied against USENET postings in addition to regular Web sites, and another service called DejaNews offers even more functionality for searching through the enormous volume of USENET postings. For example, the site archives newsgroup contributions, and you can search them by keyword, and then track click through the rest of the threaded discussion. A search of contributions using the keyword "psychology" resulted in over 16,000 hits, so you will need to practice for a while to get the hang of searching newsgroup postings. You can also view a variety of statistics and profiles, such as one that provides data on the number of postings

Your Electronic Persona

Online, people form impressions about you based on what you type. It's a leveling experience, and your good looks, athletic body, beautiful smile, sophisticated accent, and charming laugh are all irrelevant. Even with such limited information about each participant, impressions are definitely formed, using cues such as the content of your message, the frequency of your postings, your use of foul language, and the number of typos and misspellings.

Your e-mail address also says something about you. Many students and faculty have an e-mail address that indicates their institution, and people will use that to form impressions. Those who obtain their e-mail account through a commercial online service will also be identifiable through their address (e.g., aol.com, compuserve.com, prodigy.com). The user name you carry, on the left of the @ sign, might also lead to impressions. In many cases, your user name will be automatically assigned to you following the conventions of your provider. At universities, for example, one convention is to use the first initial plus the first seven digits of the last name. Some services let you choose any name you like, as long as it's unique on their service. If you frivolously choose *bigbird* or *tufdude*, your discussion group associates will draw their own conclusions about your personality.

Many people like to add "emotikons" to their postings to add a more human dimension to their electronic persona. These "emotional icons" use symbols available on a keyboard to express some emotion. Some widely understood ones are :) (smiling), :((frowning), and ;) (winking). Emotikons, some of which are quite elaborate and go on for several lines, are invented on a daily basis through the creativity of people who want to express themselves online. If you use these frequently, though, you might appear to be rather emotional.

Several widely used abbreviations are also in use in online conversations. Examples include IMHO (in my humble opinion), BTW (by the way), and FWIW (for what it's worth). Innovations on the Internet are allowing people to choose their own avatars, or graphical images, when they participate in online chats, discussion groups, or virtual reality environments. As this technology improves, it will be fascinating to see how people use it to present electronic personae to the world.

a particular author contributed to each newsgroup over a period of time. The service (http://www.dejanews.com/) is free.

Online CHAT

Synchronous conversations in which people hold live keyboard-based chatting sessions are available on the Internet and the commercial online services. Internet Relay Chat (irc) may be available on your host, and it is one of the most popular real-time conversation systems. (Many academic hosts do not offer irc access because it lacks educational value and can be a major timesink for students.) Conversations are held on "channels" with names like #hottub, #Socialism, #mermaid, and #camelot. Web-based chatting systems are also available. The Internet also supports audio conversations for those with multimedia computers and microphones. There are some psychology-related support groups that make good use of online chatting systems, and you can find out more about these when you join mailing groups or newsgroups that use them.

Psych Online Icons

This book uses several icons to show at a glance the kind of resource for each entry. Many resources merit more than one icon because the contents are heterogeneous or available through several methods. A special icon designates particularly valuable resources in psychology. This is reserved for only the very best, judged by depth; breadth; and importance to psychology students, faculty, and practitioners.

World Wide Web

You can access these through a graphical Web browser such as Netscape Navigator or Internet Explorer. The URL is provided.

Books and Journals

Materials with significant text-based content, such as online journals and electronic library resources, carry the book icon.

CD-ROM

The CD-ROM icon indicates that the resource is distributed in this format by the vendor. For most of these resources, you will need a CD-ROM drive on your computer. Some library resources and databases distributed on CD-ROM may be available on your university's library network.

ftp

File Transfer Protocol

The ftp icon indicates that resources can be obtained via anonymous ftp. If you need to change to a specific directory when you reach the ftp site, the information will be included. If you're using a graphical Web browser, the software will usually handle the details for you if you type the URL (such as ftp://hostname/pub/). If you're using a text interface, you can reach the correct location by typing ftp, followed by the hostname at the command line.

tel

Telnet

A few resources in this book require you to telnet to a particular host computer. The procedures you use to establish a telnet session with a remote host vary depending on the kind of software you're using. With a graphical Web browser, for example, you can usually configure the preferences on the browser software so you can launch the telnet client application from the browser. With a text interface, you would enter telnet, followed by the hostname at the command line to reach your destination.

Gopher

Although now nearly extinct, the few gopher sites are identified by the rodent icon, the mascot of the University of Minnesota, where the software was developed.

Mailing Lists

The many mailing lists are identified with one of these two mailbox icons, indicating low volume, or moderate to high. For the very-high-volume lists, you might use the DIGEST option if it is available unless you like frequent interruptions.

Software

Software resources are identified with the floppy disk, and this icon will point to psychology-related software available through commercial distributors, software developers, faculty,

Netiquette Guidelines for Online Discussion Groups

The best way to understand what is appropriate in a particular mailing list or newsgroup is to read any usage guidelines carefully and read the frequently asked questions (FAQ) file if there is one. The FAQ will explain the focus of the group and rules for participating, and it will be reposted periodically so that newcomers don't miss it. You should also listen and lurk for a while before jumping into the conversation. Netiquette is critical for these groups to survive and flourish because improper postings sour the group for others who may then drop out. Flame wars are not common in most of the resources in this book, but they do occur and they diminish the value of the group for the other participants. Some netiquette basics are

ψ Stay on the group's subject.
ψ Send e-mail privately to a fellow participant if the discussion isn't relevant to the group.
ψ Respect the decisions of the moderator, and be patient when a group has technical difficulties or delays.
ψ Avoid cross-postings.
ψ If you disagree with a person's statements, argue your point without hurling personal insults.
ψ Don't use the discussion group for commercial purposes.

Some special rules apply to mailing lists to avoid deluging the participants with unwanted mail and wasting their time:

ψ Don't send mail to the mailing list address unless it is information you want the whole group to read.
ψ Be sure your e-mail system is not sending automated receipt confirmations to the whole mailing list.
ψ If you reply to a single posting in a digest containing many postings, don't include the whole digest in your reply – delete what you don't need.

If you're interested in the psychological dynamics of electronic communication, you might check out the mailing lists called NETDYNAM and RESEARCH in chapter 5.

researchers, downloads, or online software repositories. The text will explain how to obtain the software and platform requirements.

USENET Newsgroups
The newspaper icon is used to identify newsgroups available through USENET, arranged in hierarchies.

Videos/films
Resources that offer videos or extensive video databases are identified by the movie icon.

POL-STAR

Finally, the **P**sych **On**line POL-STAR identifies resources of exceptional quality and utility. Criteria for the POL-STAR rating include depth, breadth, overall quality, relevance to psychology, original content, sophistication, and input from reviewers and colleagues. Remember, though, that many of these resources are growing quickly and their developers have ambitious goals. Also, judgments (and biases) about what is really useful will vary, depending on your interests. Some of the very specialized resources may be exactly what you're looking for, POL-STAR or no POL-STAR. Nevertheless, exploring computer-based and online resources is time-consuming, so, if you can't leisurely explore the resources in this guide, the POL-STAR will guide you to some very fine materials.

Glossary

anonymous ftp – The procedure used to log in to another computer without needing an account, especially to copy files. Use "anonymous" as the login name and your e-mail address as the password.

ASCII file – Text-only file containing no special formatting codes or characters; abbreviation stands for American Standard Code for Information Exchange.

BBS – Bulletin Board System.

binary file – Computer files such as programs, images, videoclips, sound files, formatted word-processing files, and others that include more than ASCII text.

cross-posting – Sending the same message to multiple mailing lists or newsgroups.

digest – A compilation of the messages that have been posted to a mailing list over a period of time, usually at least a day.

e-journal – A scholarly journal distributed electronically, often through mailing lists or newsgroups or on the Web.

ftp – File transfer protocol, which allows you to connect to a different host and transfer files between hosts.

gopher – Menu-driven application used to access Internet resources organized in hierarchical menus.

graphical Web browser – Software such as Netscape Navigator, Internet Explorer, Mosaic, and others that allows users to access Web sites and interpret the graphical and multimedia elements.

home page – A Web site for an organization, a company, a university, or an individual.

HTML – Hypertext Markup Language, used to create pages for the World Wide Web.

hypertext – A system of creating materials for online use that takes advantage of links within and between files and hosts; users can jump from one link to the next, using the keyboard or mouse.

Internet Relay Chat (irc) – A system that supports real-time text-based conversations on the Internet.

Internet Service Provider (ISP) – A company or an organization that provides Internet access to customers through dial-up or direct connections.

list owner – The individual responsible for managing a mailing list.

LISTSERV – Software used to manage mailing lists.

lurking – Reading messages in a discussion forum without participating. This practice is advisable when you first join a group.

lynx – Software used to browse the World Wide Web in text mode.

Mailbase – An organization in the UK that sponsors hundreds of mailing lists, using Mailbase software.

mailing list – An e-mail address that sends incoming mail out to the e-mail addresses of all subscribed participants; mailing lists generally have a specific topic and serve as discussion forums.

Majordomo – One of several kinds of software used to automate the maintenance of a mailing list.

mirror site – An Internet site that is duplicated in another geographic location to avoid transmission delays and reduce the load on the main server.

newsgroup – A discussion forum based on a distributed bulletin board system (USENET News).

newsreader – Software used to read and respond to postings in newsgroups.

node – A computer host linked to the Internet.

pkunzip.exe – Software used to decompress many files found at Internet sites that have been compressed with pkzip.exe to make them smaller and faster to transmit.

Post (or posting) – A message sent to a mailing list or newsgroup.

RAM – Random access memory.

spamming – Posting inappropriate commercial messages to multiple mailing lists, newsgroups, or other online discussion forums or sending such unsolicited messages by e-mail.

text file – A computer file containing only text characters with no special formatting. Also called ASCII file.

thread – In a discussion forum, a group of related messages on the same topic, including the original message and all the follow-up replies.

URL – Uniform Resource Locator, a standard format for identifying resources on the Internet.

USENET – The system of distributed bulletin boards called newsgroups.

VBRUN300.DLL – A file commonly available in shareware repositories that must be in the Windows directory in order to run Windows software developed in Visual Basic.

webzine – A magazine on the World Wide Web.

winzip – Windows shareware used to decompress zipped files.

zip file – A file created using compression software such as pkzip, which must be decompressed before it can be used; the file usually has the extension .zip. Some compressed files are "self-extracting," so, when you run the file, it will automatically decompress (or explode).

3 Megasites and Library Resources

Anumber of online and computer-based resources span a very wide terrain in psychology, covering numerous subdisciplines. This chapter includes the online "megasites" for psychology, the smaller but general online resources, the Web sites for psychology-related organizations, and the general library resources and databases. It also includes clearinghouses for psychology-related information, giant software collections, broad-based electronic journals, and some of the online magazines whose content spans several psychological disciplines.

Finding just the right book, article, software, or other resource can still be a struggle, even with CD-ROM databases and an enormous variety of online places to check. In fact, that is the main problem. Librarians know the value of electronic tools, perhaps more than anyone. However, there are few generally accepted standards for interfaces, searching commands, citation styles, or platform requirements.

Consider, for example, the book. This type of resource has been around for thousands of years, and there has been ample time for commonly accepted standards to develop. Librarians agree on how to catalog them so people can understand what is in the book, when it was published, who wrote it, and where to obtain a copy. When you pick up a book, you expect to find certain common features. For a nonfiction book, for example, you'll find a title page, a copyright notice in standard format, a table of contents, an ISBN, and an index. You expect the pages to be numbered, and, with a few exceptions, you can expect to turn pages from right to left.

These fundamental standards haven't yet evolved for electronic resources, though the general adoption of the Uniform Resource Locator standard for resources on the Internet is a good start. If someone hands you a diskette, though, there is no standard way to access and use the material on it. You might have to decompress a file, access it through some other program, or type a:setup at the computer prompt. If you can get the program started, you have few guidelines about how to actually use it. It might have a menu somewhere on the opening screen, or it might expect you to already know commands to start working with the program. You might use the mouse or keyboard, and pressing the escape key could do any number of unpredictable things. Even accessing "help" is nonstandard. You might need a function key, the question mark, the letter *H*, or a mouse click.

The power of electronic library resources is so enormous, though, that the information-literate person can't ignore them and wouldn't want to. These resources are so important that people will put up with even the most cumbersome and idiosyncratic interfaces. The PsycINFO collection of databases, for example, is arguably the single most important electronic library resource in psychology, and its value as a searching tool is unsurpassed – provided you spend some time learning how to use it.

APA Journals Go Online

On January 1, 1998, the American Psychological Association began offering to members and affiliates online fee-based access to the journals the association publishes, which include many of the most significant in the field. Examples include

American Psychologist
Behavioral Neuroscience
Developmental Psychology
Journal of Applied Psychology
Journal of Counseling Psychology
Journal of Personality and Social Psychology
Psychology and Aging

This new service is a great convenience for students, teachers, and researchers, saving them countless trips to the library and hours at the photocopier. Gary VandenBox, APA publisher, says that it took all of 1997 to digitize APA journal articles published from 1995 to 1997, "so we had a three-year backfile to put up on January 1, 1998, and we have added the 1998 issues as they are available." Fortunately for the Web team, he says, "the APA Journals program already exists, publishing 35 APA and Educational Publishing Foundation journals. All of this involves 5,000 authors, 12,000 reviewers, 100 editors and associate editors, and 50 in-house technical production staff. The movement of the APA Journals into an electronic environment only took another five people, but they could not have done it without the many, many people already contributing their share."

Because of the full-text availability of journals, usage of the APA Web site doubled. "We are now receiving over a half million hits per week, which is around 2,250,000 per month." Details about fees and access can be found at the APA's Web site (www.apa.org) in the Member's Area.

American Association for the Advancement of Science (AAAS)
http://www.aaas.org/

The Web site of AAAS offers the full text of some its articles (fee-based) and access to various scientific databases, other Web sites, and several ongoing discussion forums about science policy issues. AAAS has a service for posting news about research findings to establish a streamlined means of communicating this information to science reporters and the public. The service is at http://www.eurekalert.org, and instructions are available online.

American Psychological Society
http://psych.hanover.edu/APS/

The American Psychological Society maintains a Web site housed at Hanover College, which includes links to databases for research funding, electronic journals, lists of discussion groups, and a software archive. The society was founded in 1988 and is dedicated to the advancement of psychological science and the giving away of psychology in the public interest.

Announcement of Psychology Conferences
sci.psychology.announce

This moderated newsgroup accepts and posts announcements from organizations about conferences, workshops, internships, new journals, and other notable events and resources.

Annual Reviews
http://www.annurev.org/

Annual Reviews publishes several important series for a number of disciplines, several of which are very useful to psychology students (e.g., *Annual Review of Psychology, Annual Review of Neuroscience, Annual Review of Sociology*). These books are useful resources for psychology students and professionals wishing to obtain an overall review of research in a particular subfield. This Web site allows you to search abstracts from the past five years by title or author. It also has a searchable bibliography for the years 1984-95.

APA's PsycNet
http://www.apa.org/

The home Web site of the American Psychological Association is a true megasite, and it is a good place to start Web surfing for psychology students and professionals alike. The site is carefully and professionally written, organized, and maintained, and it offers an enormous array of resources for anyone interested in the serious study of psychology.

A major new fee-based service that recently was added to the APA Web site is the online availability of full-text APA journal articles from 1995 to the present for members and affiliates (see box). The articles are searchable via a quick search or a more comprehensive field-restricted search, and, in addition, journals can be browsed by title. You'll need your eight-digit member ID and your password to gain access to the articles.

Free services offered at the APA Web site include documents on psychology for the general public; legislative news about psychology; information about undergraduate and graduate education in psychology; listings and descriptions of APA's books, journals, and conferences; information about the 50 divisions and state-affiliated associations; and information about how to become a full or associate member of the APA.

The Student Information section of this Web site is especially well done. It helps students think through the process of mapping out their future, exploring different kinds of psychology-related careers and educational paths to reach them.

The site also includes selected articles and the classified position announcement ads that appear in the "APA Monitor," the monthly newspaper of the APA. Of particular interest to students are the sections announcing special opportunities and awards, such as the Summer Science Institute.

PsycNet offers topical and timely material on current events related to psychology. If you become a regular visitor to PsycNet, you might want to take advantage of its URL-Minder service through which you will receive e-mail whenever the site is updated. Fortunately, the site is searchable by keyword – a very useful feature in a site so large.

The Atlantic Monthly
http://www.theatlantic.com/

The Atlantic Monthly's Web presence is called Atlantic Unbound, and it provides access to an electronic version of its respected magazine, with occasional articles related to psychology.

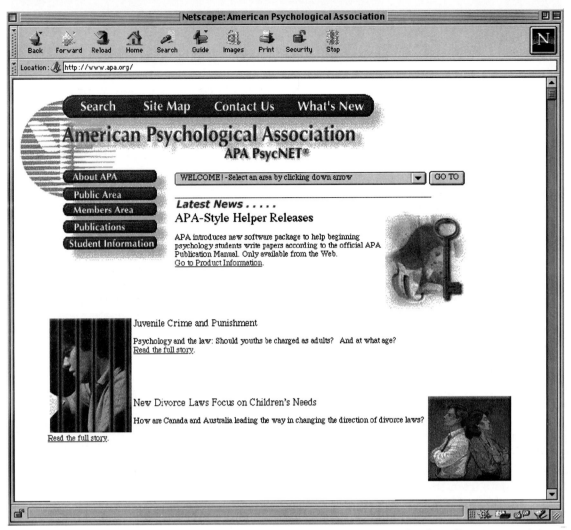

Behavioral and Brain Sciences (BBS) Target Article Reprints

http://www.princeton.edu/~harnad/bbs.html

Published by Cambridge University Press, the interdisciplinary BBS offers articles in psychology, neurosciences, behavioral biology, cognitive science, artificial intelligence, linguistics, and philosophy, along with peer commentaries on each of the articles.

The Canadian Journal of Behavioural Science

http://www.cpa.ca/cjbsnew/

The Canadian Journal of Behavioural Science publishes original contributions in the applied areas of psychology, including abnormal psychology, psychotherapy, developmental psychology, clinical psychology, community psychology, and others. The site includes full-text articles of recent issues.

Canadian Psychological Association
http://www.cpa.ca

This well-designed Web site offers information on careers, book releases, government regulations, and CPA documents and links to journal articles. Material is presented in both English and French.

Contemporary Applied Psychology in Spain (Psicologia Aplicada Contemporanea en España)
http://www.ucm.es/OTROS/Psyap/hispania/

The site provides links to articles about the study and practice of psychology in Spain.

Discussions on Psychology
alt.psychology

This unmoderated newsgroup in the alt top-level category is an open-ended discussion of topics from serial killers to scientology. Participants digress, lose their tempers, fire off sarcastic comments, and occasionally engage in some meaningful conversation. The newsgroup has many cross-postings.

ERIC
(Educational Resources Information Center)
http://www.aspensys.com/eric/

Supported by the U.S. Department of Education, Office of Educational Research and Improvement, and National Library of Education, ERIC is an excellent resource for students, educators, and educational psychologists. The ERIC database includes more than 950,000 abstracts of documents and articles on educational research from around the world and is available on CD-ROM. ERIC also offers the ERIC Digests, two-page research summaries written by experts in the field on specific topics, searchable by keywords and very popular with students and researchers. ERIC's home page has links to its other sponsored activities, such as the National Parent Information Network and the National Library of Education.

The work for creating the ERIC database is done in subject-specific clearinghouses, which collect, abstract, and index the materials in specific subject areas. Several clearinghouses deal with psychology-related materials, such as the following:

ERIC Clearinghouse on Assessment and Evaluation
http://ericae.net/

Housed at Catholic University of America, this site includes information about the clearinghouse and a wealth of other services as well. Access to the digests, to the ERIC database, and to related services is available.

ERIC Clearinghouse on Counseling and Student Services
http://www.uncg.edu/~ericcas2/

This clearinghouse began at the University of Michigan but is now located at University of North Carolina at Greensboro in the School of Education. It offers virtual libraries with full-text collections of resources on topics such as school violence, cultural diversity, and school-to-work transition.

ERIC Clearinghouse on Elementary and Early Childhood Education
http://ericeece.org

University of Illinois Urbana-Champaign is the home of this clearinghouse for ERIC, which deals with social, cognitive, emotional, and educational issues of childhood.

ERIC Clearinghouse on Languages and Linguistics
http://www.cal.org/ericcll/

Operated by the Center for Applied Linguistics, a private nonprofit organization, this clearinghouse focuses on languages and language education, English as a second language, bilingualism, intercultural communication and cultural education, and study abroad programs. The center is also the home of the clearinghouse for ESL Literacy Education.

ERIC Clearinghouse for Social Studies/Social Science Education
http://www.indiana.edu/~ssdc/
eric_chess.html

Located at Indiana University, this clearinghouse deals with the educational literature in the social studies. Adjunct clearinghouses on law-related education and United States-Japan studies are also housed here.

Family Studies Database
National Information Services Corporation
Wyman Towers
3100 St. Paul St.
Baltimore, MD 21218
(410) 243-0797
http://www.nisc.com

A database of more than 185,000 bibliographic entries and abstracts on social science research on domestic violence, family law, work and gender issues, and sexual behavior. The National Information Services Corporation publishes a number of psychology-related databases in addition to the one on family studies, and information about subscriptions can be found at its Web site.

General Discussion of Psychology
sci.psychology.misc

This open newsgroup is extremely active and, partly because it is not moderated, includes a grab bag of postings that range from the sublime to the ridiculous. The freewheeling, sometimes-acerbic conversation is informal and many psychology students share their experiences and queries in this forum. It also includes announcements of various kinds, from new Web sites to alternative therapies, as well as the ever-present cross-postings.

Human-Computer Interaction Bibliography
http://www.hcibib.org/

The site is a free-access bibliography on human-computer interaction. It provides access to abstracts of journal issues links to other Web sites and a mailing list about human-computer interaction.

iec *Pro*GAMMA
http://indy1.gamma.rug.nl/sibweb/iechomfr.html

The "iec" stands for Interuniversity Expertise Center, and ProGAMMA's goal is to stimulate the development and distribution of innovative software related to the social and behavioral sciences. The center provides assistance and advice in software development, publishes newsletters and brochures, and organizes international conferences called Social Science Information Technology. The center is supported by the Dutch government and several universities in northern Europe. One very valuable service offered through iec ProGAMMA is SIByl, listed later in this chapter.

The Internet Public Library
http://ipl.org/

In 1995, the School of Library and Information Sciences at the University of Michigan sponsored a prototype electronic public library on the Internet, with a reference desk, youth services, a section on education, and services for librarians and information professionals. It has now matured and is its own grant-supported entity. Look under Reference, then Social Science, to find psychology materials and links. Psychology resources are not extensive, but the project demonstrates how regular library services can be provided on the Internet.

InterPsych
http://www.shef.ac.uk/uni/projects/ gpp/index.html

InterPsych, a nonprofit cyberorganization started by Ian Pitchfield at the University of Sheffield, supports a large collection of psychology-related mailing lists. It is an international confederation of organizations for health, behavior, cognition, and education. The span of interests is wide, and members invite professionals to join them in developing Web resources, new mailing lists, electronic journals, and new projects. The chief aims of InterPsych are to foster interdisciplinary debate and empirical collaboration on the topic of psychopathology, and to encourage the use of Internet resources by academics and clinical practitioners.

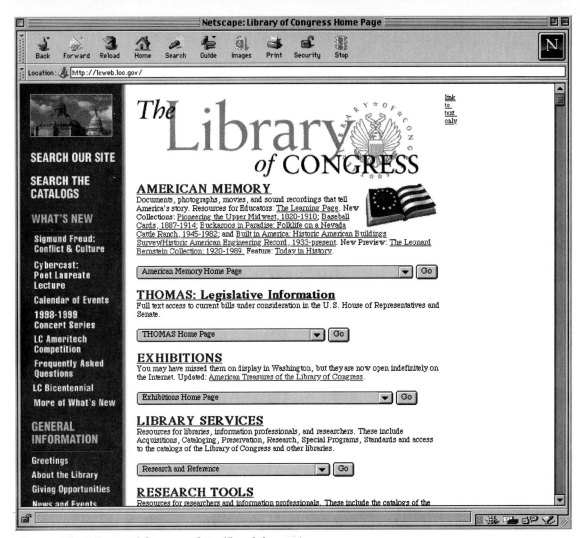

Source: The Library of Congress (http://lcweb.loc.gov).

INTROPSY
Send e-mail to
LISTSERV@VM.Tulsa.cc.ok.us
Put in the body of the message:
SUBSCRIBE INTROPSY Yourname

http://www.tulsa.oklahoma.net/~jnichols/
stulists.html
This is a mailing list for undergraduate students to discuss academic issues in introductory psychology. It is not a support forum. Faculty are welcome to subscribe but should keep in mind that the list is primarily for students.

Recent discussions have covered adrenaline, neurons, teenage pregnancy, and the correlation between churchgoing and crime.

Look for future lists from this server pertaining to other topics in undergraduate psychology: social psychology, introductory statistics, personality, etc.

Journal of Applied Behavior Analysis
http://www.envmed.rochester.edu/
wwwrap/behavior/jaba/jabahome.htm
Includes a searchable database of tables of contents of current and previous issues, with abstracts. The site also offers hypertext reprints of complete articles from the journal. Follow the links to reach the *Journal of the Experimental*

Analysis of Behavior, with the same kind of functionality at the Web site.

Journal of Mind and Behavior
http://kramer.ume.maine.edu/~jmb/
The journal focuses on interdisciplinary approaches to psychology and related fields, with articles exploring consciousness, the mind/body problem, methodological issues, social philosophy, and related areas. The Web site includes abstracts.

Library of Congress
http://lcweb.loc.gov/

Library of Congress MARVEL
gopher://marvel.loc.gov/ [being phased out]
The Library of Congress offers an enormous range of resources to scholars, professionals, librarians, students, and anyone else looking for books, videos, films, copyright information, information about legislation, digital collections, exhibits, and government activities. The site maintains a vast catalog of all the books in the library, a resource so valuable that it will be well worth your while to struggle through the cumbersome interface. You can't check out any books, of course, but you will find out what materials have been published on your topic, including the most obscure. The American Memory project, featured at this site, is a groundbreaking attempt to present photographs, movies, and sound recordings that describe American history. The site also includes a database of legislative activities and one on copyrights. Some of the library's materials can also be accessed via anonymous ftp to ftp.loc.gov.

Links to Psychological Journals
http://www.shef.ac.uk/~psysc/journals/journals.html

US mirror site: http://telehealth.net/armin/
Armin Günther of Augsburg, Germany, has created this searchable database of more than 1,000 psychology-related journals with mirror sites in Australia, Germany, Great Britain and Japan. You can search journal titles alphabetically, by language (English, German, French, Dutch, and Spanish), and by keywords. The site links to these journals, which provide general information, tables of contents, and some abstracts, but few full-text articles. To find full-text articles, Günther has created a PsychArticleSearch feature, which searches articles in one journal only or in groups of journals.

National Library of Medicine
http://www.nlm.nih.gov/
The U.S. National Library of Medicine's home Web site is a treasure trove of book catalogs, databases, brochures, lists of events, descriptions of health-related funding initiatives, and many other resources. It offers free access to several databases, the most important of which is MEDLINE, which has more than nine million citations. Others include Clinical Alerts (early release of clinical information from the National Institutes of Health); AIDS-related databases; HSTAT (full text of clinical practice guidelines); and the NLM Locator (an online catalog of the library's holdings). This site features some innovative multimedia exhibits, such as the Visible Human Project, and an exhibition featuring images of medicine in art and history.

Nature
http://www.nature.com/

Mirror site in the U.S.:
http://www.america.nature.com/
    Nature is a weekly international science journal, covering science news, scientific articles, databases of products, and some full-text articles that have appeared in *Nature*'s editions. The complete full-text online journal will be available soon to subscribers. The site also has position vacancy announcements. The first site listed is in the United Kingdom, the second in the United States. Connect to whichever is closest to you.

New England Journal of Medicine On-line
http://www.nejm.org/
    The online version of this widely respected weekly medical journal includes the full text of many of the features and columns, abstracts of the articles, and, for subscribers, the fulltext of the complete journal, including archives.

Online Computer Library Center, Inc. (OCLC)
(800) 848-5878
http://www.oclc.org/
    This organization offers computer-based products and services to libraries and educational institutions around the world, including online and CD-ROM services for cataloging, collection development, interlibrary loan, and reference materials. Examples of some of its products include the Online Union Catalog, which is an enormous bibliographic database used by libraries for cataloging purposes, and FirstSearch, which is an online reference service that enables access to dozens of databases for library staff and patrons. Another service is Electronic Journals Online (EJO), which provides access to the full text of some peer-reviewed research journals. OCLC is at the forefront of efforts to provide tools for electronic scholarship.

Psychiatry On-Line
http://www.ccspublishing.com/j_psych.htm
    This journal boasts that it is the first electronic medical journal fully available online. Current price is $9.95 per year for all materials, including e-mail updates. Psychiatrists, and those interested in psychiatry, are the primary audience, and submissions are refereed. Some accompanying services offered by the publisher are available only by paid subscription.

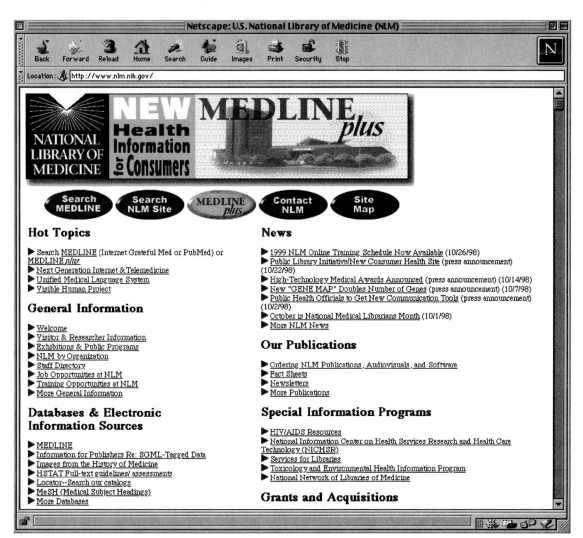

Source: U.S. National Library of Medicine (http://www.nlm.nlm.nih.gov).

PsychREF™

http://maple.lemoyne.edu/~hevern/
psychref.html

Vincent Hevern at LeMoyne College has created a megasite filled with Internet psychology resources. Although its audience was students enrolled at LeMoyne, students, professors, and professionals in the field will find this site clearly organized and incredibly useful. Section titles are General Resources; Teaching & Scholarly Activities by Faculty; Resources for Students & Academic Advisors; and Topics and Subfields in Psychology. Hevern kindly announces that he'll be on sabbatical for the 98/99 year, so the site may not be updated regularly.

PsycINFO

http://www.apa.org/psycinfo/

PsycLIT CD-ROM

PSYCINFO

Send e-mail to LISTSERV@LISTS.APA.ORG
Put in the body of the message:
SUBSCRIBE PSYCINFO Yourname

PsycINFO is the department at the American Psychological Association responsible for some of the most important research tools for psychologists and psychology students. It publishes the well-known *Psychological Abstracts*, which, since 1927, has been providing bibliographic references and abstracts to articles in all the major (and many of the minor) psychology journals of the world. Articles are screened to ensure they meet the criterion of psychological relevance. PsycINFO began developing computerized bibliographies in the 1960s. It now offers electronic products, such as a Web-based version of PsycINFO, and several CD-ROM subsets.

The PsycINFO database is the computerized mother lode, with entries going back to 1887 and more than 4,000 new references added each month. Each PsycINFO reference includes the bibliographic citation and publishing information, a summary or abstract of the content, and standardized keyword indexing, which helps researchers find the article.

The APA offers many routes by which psychologists and psychology students can access the comprehensive version of PsycINFO on the Web or its smaller and less comprehensive derivatives. Many universities have developed leasing agreements with APA so that students and faculty can use the whole database or smaller subsets. PsycFirst, for example, which includes references from the most recent three years, can be accessed through the FirstSearch system from Online Computer Library Center (OCLC), if your institution has made arrangements. Before contacting any of the commercial online services to gain access to PsycINFO or its subsets, check with your reference librarian to see if he or she has one of these institutional leases.

PsycINFO also produces CD-ROMs that are purchased by libraries all over the world and are either placed on their networks or checked out to students to use inside the library. These contain subsets of the PsycINFO database. PsycLIT on CD-ROM covers journal articles from 1887 to the present.

Another addition to the PsycINFO family of products is a mailing list called, not surprisingly, PsycINFO. The list is designed to provide a forum for discussing effective search strategies, new products, and other specific issues related to the PsycINFO databases.

APA members and student affiliates with paid-up dues who have purchased at least one subscription to an APA print journal can also access the PsycINFO database by purchasing a subscription to the online product. See http://www.apa.org, Members Area, for details.

PSYCOLOQUY
http://www.princeton.edu/~harnad/psyc.html

PSYCOLOQUY
Send e-mail to
LISTSERV@PUCC.PRINCETON.EDU
Put in the body of the message:
SUBSCRIBE PSYC Yourname

(Mirrored in:
sci.psychology.journals.psycoloquy)

PSYCOLOQUY is a refereed electronic journal sponsored by the American Psychological Association on an experimental basis. There is no hard copy version. It publishes articles, brief reports, book reviews, and commentary in almost all areas of psychology. A chief goal, one that is very well served by its medium, is to distribute ideas and findings quickly so the researcher can obtain immediate feedback from colleagues around the world.

You can access this journal in a number of ways. It is available at the Web site listed above and on USENET as a moderated newsgroup (sci.psychology.journals.psycoloquy). Finally, you can subscribe to it so it will be delivered to your e-mail address in the same way you subscribe to mailing lists.

Psyc Site

http://www.stange.simplenet.com/
psycsite

Ken Stange of the University of Nipissing in Ontario, Canada, developed a site that emphasizes links to scientific resources in psychology. It has links to other Web sites sorted by subject, a listing of mailing lists and news groups, links to sources to download software, and other resource pointers. The site has a number of psychologists who have volunteered to answer e-mail questions for people who have hit dead ends in their research on particular questions. Volunteers to be experts are solicited. One excellent feature of this site is a research center where professionals can link their research project to recruit subjects and where one can volunteer to be such a subject.

PsyJourn

(408) 257-8131
http://www.shrinktank.com/

The original bulletin board known as Shrink Tank was started in 1983 on a Commodore 64 computer and run by Rob Bischoff. It has now become a Web site called PsyJourn, emphasizing self-help as an adjunct to therapy. It features psychology and mental health software, most of which is shareware, and many links to psychology-related resources on the Internet.

PsyLink

http://www.psych.neu.edu/psylink
The Department of Psychology at Northeastern University has created this megasite with links to journals, associations, worldwide psychology departments, and every branch of psychology.

Within each branch, links are divided into categories such as

Conferences, Meetings, and Workshops; Newsgroups and Mailing Lists; People; and Software & Code.

Research and Discussion About Mistakes

alt.psychology.mistake-theory

Apparently, few mistakes are made in psychology, or, if they are, they aren't posted to this forum. The unmoderated newsgroup generally contains only the innumerable, irrelevant cross-postings from other psychology-related newsgroups. It's a relatively new addition, though, so perhaps some intriguing material will turn up.

Research Issues in Psychology

sci.psychology.research
http://www.grohol.com/psychart.htm

This high-quality, research-oriented newsgroup is moderated, and postings may take three days for review before they appear. Messages tend to be longer and academic, focusing on general research issues and announcements of new journals or related Web sites. Some articles use APA citation style. Many participants are academic psychologists in university settings, and the topics might include research on the Internet, APA publication style, or research methodologies in specific disciplines. The guidelines for participation are posted weekly and are available at the Web site mentioned. Not surprisingly, the number of postings to this group is far less than that of most of the other psychology-related newsgroups, but the quality is higher and the group is mercifully relieved from the endless, redundant cross-postings. A recent thread dealt with a discussion on the use of computer-assisted interviewing techniques.

Scientific American

http://www.sciam.com

The *Scientific American* Web site offers the full text of most articles back to 1996 up to the current issue. Under Ask the Experts, you can send in a scientific question and hope for a published response from one of the scientists who participate in the program. A recent query from Australia, for example, asked whether the human race is evolving or devolving.

SIByl: The Social Science Software Databank

http://www.gamma.rug.nl/
sibhome.html

SIByl is the Software Information Bank of iec ProGAMMA, and it contains detailed descriptions of computer applications used in the social and behavioral sciences, including purchasing information and reviews, if any are available. The collection is searchable by means of the SIByl Search Tool, which allows indexed or full-text searching. Software authors and publishers can submit information about their products to the SIByl database online. Many of the products listed in the SIByl database are research-oriented and quite expensive, but the collection also includes some software under $100. With its European base, the list initially had few entries from North American publishers, but these are growing rapidly. Demos of some of the products are available for downloading.

SIMSOC

Send e-mail to
MAILBASE@MAILBASE.AC.UK
Put in the body of the message:
JOIN SIMSOC Yourname

Here is a mailing list with a very specific audience – those interested in the use of computer simulation in the social sciences. This is a growing field, so the SIMSOC list is the place to learn about cutting-edge topics, including approaches based on micro-simulation and multi-agent modeling. Members also help each other with resources and advice.

Social Science Information Gateway (SOSIG)

http://sosig.esrc.bris.ac.uk/

This Web site provides links to social science educational and research resources around the Internet and a searchable database for finding the appropriate resources for your needs. The links emphasize quality over quantity and are not comprehensive. Each resource listed has a paragraph description, a list of keywords by which the resource has been cataloged, and a link to the resource itself.

SuperPsychNet

http://users.aol.com/warmgeoff/homepage.html

SuperPsychNet was created by Geoffrey Warme. It is a short but helpful collection of links to other major resource sites in psychology, mental health, and research, covering hundreds of topics and thousands of links.

There is a particular focus on resources for graduate students and researchers, with sites such as: Research Randomizer, Online Journals, and Grant Guides. Biological psychology is also a featured topic.

Geoffrey Warme welcomes suggestions for new links, so it is always worth a visit to see what he has added.

Theories of Psychology and Behavior

sci.psychology.theory

This newsgroup is unmoderated and reasonably active, covering topics such as Freudian theory, research methodology, and IQ, as well as many cross-postings from the other psychology-related newsgroups.

Thinking Allowed

http://www.thinking-allowed.com/

Jeffrey Mishlove hosts this video-oriented Web site, offering a catalog of national public television series and a video library catalog to help people find video material related to consciousness research, psychology, philosophy, personal and spiritual development, health and healing, and the intuitive arts. Information on satellite broadcasts and schedules and comments from viewers and reviewers are also available.

UnCoverWeb

http://uncweb.carl.org/

The UnCover Company is widely known for its online database in which over 17,000 periodicals are indexed, including the psychology-related journals. At this Web site you can search the databases (free of charge) using keywords, author names, or journal titles and display the titles and journal information online for your hits. UnCover also provides a document delivery service through which you can enter your billing information online and mark the articles you would like delivered via fax or mail. Although the service is not inexpensive, if you need that one article for a paper due tomorrow, the savings in time and travel may be well worth it. Many universities have accounts with UnCover so students and faculty receive discounts on articles and other services – check with your library before ordering on your own. UnCover account holders can also take advantage of the Reveal electronic alerting service and receive automatic e-mails containing the tables of contents from specified journals and the results of search strategies entered into their individual profiles. You can also access the UnCover database and related library catalogs via telnet at the address listed.

Citation Styles for Electronic Media

Professional librarians, researchers, and academic associations have spent years in debate to develop standards for citing materials found online. Unlike published articles or books, online material may disappear, change in content, or move to a new location days after the researcher cites it. Anyone looking for the citation may not be able to find it at all, or the material may have been altered by the time the next online researcher makes a visit to the site.

Another thorny issue involves the problem of identifying the document's actual location. The Uniform Resource Locator (URL) is becoming a standard on the Internet, but documents can be quite long and they have no page numbers. A researcher who wants to cite a particular quotation in a lengthy Web page has no obvious way to tell the audience where in the document the quotation occurred, so those who want to locate the source must painstakingly sift through the entire document. Other online services do not generally use URLs, anyway, so reference citations are appearing more as directions on how to find the material than as standard citations. The writer may tell the audience to use a particular keyword, for example.

Citing an old mailing list or USENET message is especially hazardous. Many of these lists have no archives, so it may not be possible to find it online at all. An author can cite a book that has gone out of print, knowing that copies are probably available somewhere. How, though, does an author cite a reference from a mailing list, suspecting that no one will ever be able to find the original material?

Citation styles for printed words and images have evolved over hundreds of years, and a huge infrastructure exists, ensuring that people who want to find them can locate the material. Card catalogs, subject coding systems, bibliographies, the Library of Congress system, and the Dewey Decimal system are all available to help researchers locate the original source. Guidelines for the structure of citations exist for many disciplines, including psychology. These standards have come a long way since the publication of the first edition of *Psych Online*, and the emphasis is always on crediting the author's work and enabling the reader to find the material. What is needed now are standards for citing online material, ones that stress the ingredients needed for researchers to find it again, if at all possible. The *Publication Manual of the American Psychological Association*, 4th edition, contains some guidelines for citing electronic media, though it points out that standards are in the evolutionary stage.

Bibliographic Formats for Citing Electronic Information
http://www.uvm.edu/~ncrane/estyles/
Web Extension to American Psychological Association Style
http://www.beadsland.com/weapas/

Two other important sources for information about online citations are the Web sites referenced above. The first one is by Xia Li and Nancy B. Crane, authors of *Electronic Styles: A Handbook to Citing Electronic Information*, published in 1996. The second describes a proposed standard for referencing online documents in scientific publications that offers alternatives and extensions to the APA guidelines. WEAPAS invites comments and maintains a mailing list for discussion.

U.S. Government Printing Office
http://www.access.gpo.gov/

The home page of the Government Printing Office contains a searchable index of the Congressional Record and full text since 1994. Also present is the Federal Register. You need an account to access these services; call (202) 512-1530.

U.S. National Archives and Records Administration (NARA)
http://www.nara.gov/

The National Archives has a storehouse of material, though the cataloging of it is somewhat frustrating. Its Web site contains extensive information on the kinds of records maintained by NARA at the archive buildings in and around Washington, D.C., as well as those in other parts of the country. The Web site has some interesting features, such as a section on the digital classroom. Exhibits also abound, and some of them might be interesting to psychology students. One exhibit features an analysis of persuasion tactics, with many posters from World War II designed to change attitudes, encourage enlistment, and motivate citizens to buy war bonds.

4 General Resources for Students and Faculty

Some of the most inventive computer-based and online resources have been developed specifically to support the teaching and learning of psychology. This chapter covers mailing lists in which psychology students around the world congregate, software for the introductory psychology course, online resources for high school psychology faculty, an extremely active mailing list for psychology faculty, and many other items. The element that links the entries in this group is that they are all primarily for the education environment, rather than for specialized disciplines or practitioners. More specialized resources, which will also be of interest to faculty and students, are found in later chapters.

Annenberg/CPB Projects
http://www.learner.org/

The home Web site of the Annenberg/CPB Projects offers access to information about their course materials, distance learning resources, multimedia catalogs, research reports, and guidelines for faculty interested in submitting grant applications. The Annenberg/CPB Projects have sponsored the development of many psychology-related materials, such as the telecourses called *Discovering Psychology, The World of Abnormal Psychology, The Brain, Growing Old in a New Age, Seasons of Life,* and the CD-ROM called *BioQUEST.*

CTI Centre for Psychology
http://ctipsych.york.ac.uk/inst/ctipsych/

CTI-PSYCHOLOGY
Send e-mail to
MAILBASE@MAILBASE.AC.UK
Put in the body of the message:
JOIN CTI-PSYCHOLOGY Yourname

The CTI Centre for Psychology is supported by the UK Higher Education Funding Councils and focuses on the use of computers within the teaching of psychology. Its Web site offers a variety of resources to psychology students, including a list of software with descriptions and purchasing information. Software is sorted by topical category and ranges from the free software provided to faculty who adopt certain texts, to the expensive bibliographic CD-ROMs. Many of the entries list United Kingdom sources and pricing for the software, since this is a UK-based server.

CTI also operates a mailing list through Mailbase, targeted to psychology lecturers using educational technology. The list sends out relevant information from the CTI Centre for Psychology and circulates questions from participants to psychology departments in the United Kingdom. CTI-PSYCHOLOGY is a sublist of the Mailbase superlist CTI-ALL, and subscribers will automatically receive general postings from the superlist.

Classics in the History of Psychology

http://www.yorku.ca/dept/psych/classics/

Christopher D. Green of York University, Toronto, Ontario, is the editor of this large repository of full-text, historically significant documents about psychology, such as What Is Emotion? by William James, first published in a 1884 edition of *Mind*. Texts can be browsed by author, by date of publication, and by topic. Texts appear from Aristotle through present-day psychologists. Green states that the site is user-driven, so, if you'd like to see something, send him an e-mail.

Current Awareness

http://www.dpi.state.nc.us/
Crrntawrnss.form.html

North Carolina Department of Public Instruction offers online access to *Current Awareness*, a bibliography of scholarly research in education, updated monthly.

Discovering Psychology

Life Science Associates
One Fenimore Road
Bayport, NY 11705-2115
(516) 472-2111
http://www.pipeline.com/~lifesciassoc
lifesciassoc@pipeline.com

A variety of demonstrations and experiments suitable for introductory psychology are included in this set of programs for DOS, which can be purchased as a package for $495 (DOS)

or individually for $40. Topics covered include problem solving, Stroop effects, memory techniques, reinforcement schedules, consumer behavior, psychotherapy, Piaget's cognitive operations, concept formation, and others. Samples and demos are available on the Web site for download.

ELIZA

http://www-ai.ijs.si/eliza/eliza.html

Also available via anonymous ftp to:
ftp://eecs.nwu.edu/pub/eliza/

The software designed to emulate a Rogerian counselor called Eliza has been around for many years in a number of different forms, and she has emerged in a Web version at a site sponsored by the Jozef Stefan Institute in Slovenia. She asks you about your problems and uses your typed input to phrase her replies and ask for further information. This version will amuse students by the way she tactfully changes the subject when the program can't parse or evaluate the typed responses. Eliza is also available as a text-based DOS program from the ftp site referenced.

Experimental Psychology Data Simulation-Win

by J. Eckblad
Oakleaf Systems
PO Box 472
Decorah, IA 52101
(319) 382-4320
oakleaf@mboxes.com

Experiments in Perception: Evolution of a Software Program

Walter Beagley, chair of the Psychology Department at Alma College in Michigan, was intrigued by some of his students' class projects on perception and decided to write software to entice them to design their own experiments. He started out on a DEC host computer with a program that allowed students to manipulate drawings to prepare visual stimuli, using posters in the lab to help them learn how to use the program. However, he quickly appreciated the advantages of the Macintosh with its pulldown help menus and easy-to-use graphic interface. He quotes Victor Hugo, who said, "This kills that," and recognized early that the microcomputer was the fleet-footed mammal, scampering around the stodgy legs of the lumbering mainframe and minicomputer dinosaurs – at least for this kind of work. At the time, he wasn't sure whether Macintosh or Windows would be the winner in the microcomputer race and decided to write versions of his software, called *Eye Lines*, for both. Keeping up with changes in the computer industry is a constant problem for those who develop psychology-related software. After all, Walter is a psychology professor first and software developer second. However, it is often people like him, who know the most about what software really works to encourage student learning, who produce the best products. The program became publicly available in 1991 and is now used at colleges and universities in nine countries.

Relationships identified in psychological literature, particularly *Journal of Comparative Psychology*, *Journal of Experimental Psychology: General*, and *Journal of Experimental Psychology: Human Perception and Performance*, are simulated in this software (Windows, DOS, and Macintosh). Examples include optical patterns and depth perception, visual perception of lifted weight, sweetness of sugar mixtures, and size perception by children. Students or instructors can set up the experimental situation and specify the dependent variable, sample sizes, and other parameters. Twenty-five simulations are available in experimental psychology, and the company offers simulations in the area of animal behavior (e.g., male size and harem size in pinnipeds; discrimination reversal learning in fish and rats; maze learning curve for rats and ants). Simulations are $69.95 each for the first copy and $15 for additional copies; network versions and site licenses are available.

Eye Lines
by Walter Beagley
Department of Psychology
Alma College
Alma, MI 48801
(517) 463-7267
beagley@alma.edu
http://www.alma.edu/el.html

This program, available in DOS and Macintosh versions, provides a number of simulations and interactive exercises appropriate for introductory psychology or more advanced courses. It includes mirror tracing, memory exercises, rotary pursuit, a variety of visual illusions, and handwriting analysis. The experimenter can manipulate several of the variables such as the speed or distortion in the mirror-tracing task. The graphical interface takes advantage of the mouse, even with the DOS version. A six-copy license is $99.

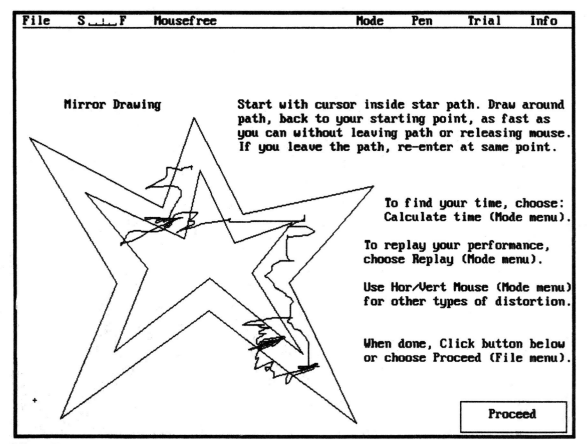

Mirror Tracing Task from Eye Lines by Wally Beagley. Reprinted by permission.

Institute for Academic Technology (IAT)
University of North Carolina at Chapel Hill
http://www.iat.unc.edu/

IAT offers a variety of resources for teachers interested in incorporating technology into their curriculum, including workshops and seminars, satellite broadcasts on subjects such as multimedia development and virtual reality, discussions on distance education, and a library of technology resources for teachers. The institute is not specifically targeted to psychology, but there are many useful materials here.

The Integrator
Brooks/Cole Publishing Company
511 Forest Lodge Road
Pacific Grove, CA 93950
(800) 487-5510
http://www.brookscole.com

The Integrator, available for introduction to psychology, for biological psychology, and for health, is a multimedia development tool that allows teachers and students to explore interactive experiments, animations, homework assignments, and video clips. Professors can use the LectureMaker feature to develop multimedia presentations. A variety of materials are included with the software, such as static images, homework assignments, animations, various demonstrations and interactive experiments, and surveys.

IPEDS Interactive Database at Arizona State University
http://129.219.88.111/ipeds/

The IPEDS Database helps you learn about the range of salaries for faculty at colleges and universities around the country. You can enter up to 24 school names at a time and the search engine will return the average salary at each for instructors through full professors. There is also a link to the list of institutions included in the database.

The database goes as far back as 1994-95 and searches for disparity between male and female salaries. Data such as these can be used for research projects or class exercises.

Job Openings in Psychology

Chronicle of Higher Education:
http://chronicle.merit.edu/.ads/.ads-by-group/.faculty/.sscience/.psychology/.links.html

APA:
http://www.apa.org:80/jobs/

American Educational Research Association (AERA):
http://tikkun.ed.asu.edu/~jobs/joblinks.html

The Graduate Education Association of Boston College:

http://www.bc.edu/bc_org/svp/st_org/gea/direct2/Ed.Empl.html

Division of Psychology, Australian National University:
http://psy.anu.edu.au/academia/psy.htm

Above are five Web sites that list job openings in psychology and are always kept current. The Chronicle's list is updated weekly, while the APA's is done monthly. The Australian National University site is also updated frequently.

AERA's site is simply a long list with some entries a few months old, but most are recent additions.

The Graduate Education Association does not offer lists of actual jobs but links to various job-listing sites around the world.

Listing of U.S. Psychology Ph.D. Programs
http://www.wesleyan.edu/spn/ranking.htm

This site ranks 185 psychology Ph.D. programs in the United States according to the results of a 1995 study conducted by the National Research Council, which emphasized overall quality. The list includes hyperlinks to the institutions' home pages if available.

MacLaboratory for Psychology: Research, 3.0
Brooks/Cole Publishing Company
511 Forest Lodge Road
Pacific Grove, CA 93950
(800) 487-5510
http://www.brookscole.com

This Macintosh CD-ROM includes an impressive and feature-rich array of simulations, exercises, and tools to provide a platform for students to design and conduct their own research in areas such as sensation and perception, motor skills, cognition, learning, social psychology, and biological psychology.

The program, created by Douglas L. Chute, emphasizes the use of the Macintosh computer as an experimental apparatus to help students learn the processes and critical thinking underlying psychological research. The detailed student manual leads students through the process of designing experiments in areas such as extrasensory perception, motor learning (mirror-tracing task), hemispheric specialization, memory span, and operant conditioning using Sniffy (described in chapter 5). The program ($360.95) also includes authoring tools for designing new experiments and stimuli.

McGraw-Hill PsyCafé
http://www.mhhe.com/socscience/intro/cafe/psycafm.htm

A virtual coffee house, PsyCafé features a wealth of resources for faculty and students in introductory psychology. Faculty can find PowerPoint lectures, teaching tips, links to research sites, ideas for class activities, a discussion forum, and an image bank with graphics that faculty can download and include in their own presentations. The "Site Builders" section features individual faculty who have developed Web sites that accompany their own psychology classes. For students, PsyCafé offers interactive exercises, psychology-related quizzes, online study help, a monthly crossword puzzle, an Internet Primer, a section on careers in psychology, and many links to other relevant sites. The Café is leasing more virtual "space" and growing constantly to provide more resources.

MegaPsych Home Page
http://www.tusla.oklahoma.net/~jnichols/megapsych.html

ftp://premier.tulsa.cc.ok.us/pub/psych/aon.txt

John W. Nichols at Tulsa Junior College in Oklahoma has created an extensive and highly valuable set of Internet resources for psychology students and faculty, including descriptions of mailing lists, e-journals, newsgroups, gopher sites, ftp sites, telnet sites, and Web pages. MegaPsych began as a simple ftp file called Addresses of Note, but now it is has grown considerably and is available through the Web at the listed address. Other categories on the site include a bookstore, a collection of articles for faculty and students of psychology, and a selection of amusing quotes relevant to human behavior. A favorite of mine, because it is so relevant to people creating psychology-related resources, is "So much to do, so little" (hang on a sec...).

MEL Lab: Experiments in Perception, Cognition, Social Psychology, and Human Factors
Psychology Software Tools
2014 Monongahela Avenue
Pittsburgh, PA 15216
(412) 271-5040
http://www.pstnet.com/

Psychology Software Tools provides a package for about $20 that includes a student textbook and DOS software with 28 classic experiments dealing with subjects such as the blind spot, serial position effect, short-term memory, prisoner's dilemma, and impression formation. Students run the experiments with themselves as subjects and see graphs of their own data. Instructor software is also available (free with the purchase of 20 student copies) that allows merging of individual student data files into a single file for the class, and the data can be exported to other statistical packages for further analysis. You will neet to order this software through your college bookstore.

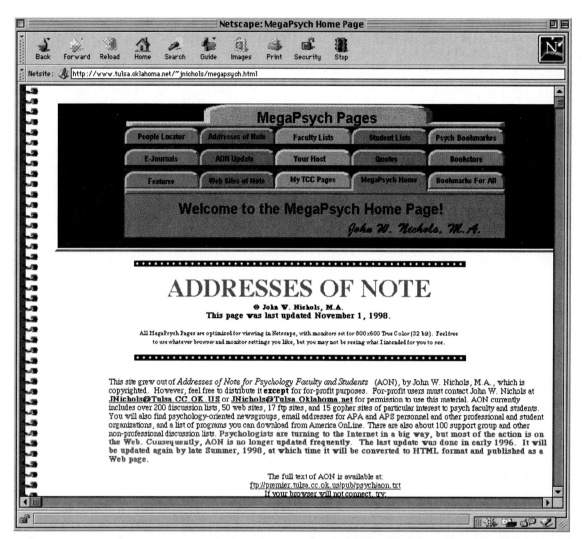

MegaPsych Home Page (http:www.tulsa.oklahoma.net/~jnichols/megapsych.html). Reprinted by permission.

Office of Teaching Resources in Psychology
http://www.lemoyne.edu/OTRP/

OTRP develops and distributes teaching and advising materials to teachers in secondary schools, colleges, and universities. Examples include information about instructional research, ethical issues in teaching, diversity issues, course syllabi, advising, and a variety of consulting services.

Online Journals
http://www.psychwatch.com/journalpage. htm

Psychwatch maintains this enormous database of online journals that is broad in scope, as well. Some journals provide full text, some only abstracts, while others require a subscription. Titles are grouped in 18 categories such as assessment, developmental psychology, forensic psychology, and cognition. There are so many titles within each category that you've probably never heard of some of them. Titles include *Counseling and Values, Decision Support Systems Journal, Journal of Melanie Klein and Object Relations,* and *CyberPsychology and Behavior.*

Online Psychology Career Center
http://www.wesleyan.edu/spn/career.htm#careerinfo

Wesleyan University's Department of Psychology sponsors this comprehensive site to provide information for the undergraduate student curious about pursuing a career in psychology. The site offers very specific advice on how to get into graduate school, prepare for the GRE, develop an academic vita, and get good letters of recommendation.

In addition to these tips, the Career Center links to job listings from the APA, such as Careers for Research-Trained Psychologists and Nonacademic Careers in Psychology, as well from a variety of other sources.

Online Survey Registration Clearinghouse
http://www.cmhc.com/research/

Conducting surveys online is efficient and cost-effective, though the population may be somewhat restricted – not everybody is surfin' the Web. However, researchers are using online surveys, and this clearinghouse provides excellent examples of what they look like. This section of the megasite Mental Health Net will be especially useful to students and faculty who may want to conduct such online research.

On a recent visit, survey topics included imaginary childhood companions; brain injury and safety: attitudes and biases; which personality types like to participate in online surveys; and, of course, cybersex.

OPAL
http://psych-www.colorado.edu:591/opal/default.htm

Mike Brezsnyak, a graduate student in clinical psychology at the University of Colorado at Boulder, has created OPAL (the Online Psychology Article Listing). It is a searchable index of online, full-text, scholarly articles on psychology, including articles that might never have been otherwise published (null results, alternative research, etc.).

Brezsnyak asks users to help him add articles to the database, either your own or those of colleagues. You can even volunteer to, as he says, " 'spider' one of the seemingly endless sites or journals that has been identified but not yet been entered into OPAL."

Projected Learning Programs, Inc.
PO Box 13060
Oklahoma City, OK 73113
(800) 248-0757
http://www.plp.com

The company offers a science and math catalog featuring a wide range of software and video resources for teachers, most of which are for K-12 or introductory college level. A few might be of interest to psychology teachers, such as the multimedia CD-ROM on Mendel's principles of heredity (PC and Macintosh) and other CD-ROMs on genetics, evolution, and animal behavior.

PRISM
Patricia M. Wallace
McGraw-Hill College

I was very proud to be involved in this team effort to create a multimedia CD-ROM with an extraordinarily rich collection of resources for psychology students, including interactive exercises, a career guide, a statistics tutorial, an

Internet primer, and a section on psychology around the globe. The sixty multimedia exercises engage the student in a wide range of psychological phenomena appropriate for the intro course using video, audio, arcade-style games, animations, psychological tests, and experiments. Several take advantage of video clips from *Candid Camera* relevant to psychology, such as the amusing segment called "Face the Rear" in which an unsuspecting elevator passenger experiences pressure to conform because the fellow "passengers" are all facing the rear. The CD-ROM, whose acronym stands for *Psychology Resources Interactive Study Media,* also includes interactive study resources with feedback on student responses geared to various McGraw-Hill texts, but the exercises and other materials can be used in any introductory course.

Projects in Experimental Psychology
Life Science Associates
One Fenimore Road
Bayport, NY 11705-2115
(516) 472-2111
lifesciassoc@pipeline.com
http://www.pipeline.com/~lifesciassoc

This suite of Windows programs includes demonstrations and simulations on topics such as visual illusions, reaction time, verbal learning, operant conditioning, maze learning, signal detection, and auditory frequency difference thresholds. The programs allow the users to manipulate various parameters and record their data for later feedback and analysis. The Level 2 group of programs requires specialized hardware available through Life Science Associates that permits the computer to function as an event recorder, a cumulative recorder, a response time analyzer and plotter, a mirror tracing device, or another typical experimental psychology lab tools.

PSYCGRAD Web Page
http://www.erols.com/matthew.simpson/psycgrad.html

PSYCGRAD
Send e-mail to LISTSERV@LISTS.APA.ORG
Put in the body of the message:
SUBSCRIBE PSYCGRAD Yourname

(Mirrored in the USENET newsgroup bit.listserv.psycgrad)

The PSYCGRAD Project is a group of resources directed to graduate students in psychology, which promotes communications, offers an electronic platform for publishing articles, and provides an electronic gateway to the many Internet-based resources in psychology. It is a well-established forum with more than 1,000 participants in countries all over the world.

The Web site provides instructions and usage guidelines on the mailing list and newsgroup options and explains how to subscribe and submit articles to the electronic publication, The Psychology Graduate Student Journal.

The project is directed toward a specific group, and, although other interested parties are welcome to read the materials, only graduate students in psychology programs are encouraged to participate. The discussion forum is not intended to be a general-purpose conversation about psychological issues. Be sure to read its mission statement (on the Web or gopher site), which contains posting and participation guidelines.

PsychLab
Queue
338 Commerce Drive
Fairfield, CT 06432
(800) 232-2224
http://www.queueinc.com

Queue distributes a variety of educational software products in subjects from early reading to English as a second language. Some have relevance to psychology teachers and students in high school or introductory college courses, particularly those from HRM Software. Examples include PsychLab (Apple), which consists of a series of experiments in perception, memory, and learning; Experiments in Human Physiology (Apple); The Body Electric (Apple or DOS); Teenage Stress Profile (Apple); and Biofeedback Microlab (Apple).

PSYCH-NEWS
Send e-mail to
LISTSERV@LISTSERV.UH.EDU
Put in the body of the message:
SUBSCRIBE PSYCH-NEWS Yourname

PSYCH-NEWS is a very active and useful discussion group primarily for teachers of psychology at the high school level. Funded by a grant from the National Science Foundation, the list is hosted by University of Houston. Discussions include teaching strategies, curriculum, advanced placement, textbooks, and grading. Many university and college faculty also belong to PSYCH-NEWS, and much information is shared between this list and TIPS.

Psψchology, an Introduction
by Martyn Long
40, Lynn Road
Gaywood, Kings Lynn
Norfolk PE30 4PX United Kingdom

This DOS freeware program from educational psychologist Martyn Long is a hypertext introduction to psychology written in the shareware authoring tool called Hypershell. It includes a rich assortment of linked material covering most of the core concepts for an introductory course. The graphic, mouse-driven interface is very easy to use, and the program has several interactive simulations on topics such as reaction time, ESP, body image, and memory. Psψchology Version 3.0 also offers a search facility to find topics quickly, graphics to illustrate concepts, and a text editor to jot down notes. The author includes a paragraph describing why he wrote this program, with a hypertext link to the topic of *intrinsic motivation.*

Psychology on a Disk
CMS Software
PO Box 1514
Columbia, MD 21044-1514
http://www.widgetworks.com/~kevin/
publishing/cms/index.html
Available in DOS or Macintosh formats for $13.50, Psychology on a Disk is a suite of 13 interactive programs for introductory psychology students. It includes simulations and experiments on topics such as the horizontal-vertical illusion, guilt detection (using a word association task), a shaping simulation, short-term memory, cognition in recall, a word game to demonstrate the AHA! insight phenomenon, the generic personality evaluation "test" with feedback to demonstrate the pitfalls of palm readers and horoscopes, a social decision-making task, and a variety of other innovative exercises suitable for the introductory psychology course.

Interactive Tutorials on the Web

John Krantz, in the Psychology Department at Hanover College in Indiana, began writing tutorials for the Web because he was intrigued by the interactive nature of the medium. Unlike printed tutorials, the Web can use hypertext, clickable image maps, multimedia, and many other features that bring psychology tutorials to life. With new programming tools for the Web emerging at blinding speed, the possibilities are endless.

His tutorials for students (http://psych.hanover.edu/Krantz/tutor.html) emphasize sensation and perception, a natural subject for an experimental psychologist who teaches these subjects. As he recruits people to contribute tutorials in other areas, he can expand the experiences of his students and enhance his own teaching expertise. The Internet opens up doors for everyone, but it's especially useful for those in small schools who have no colleagues in the same subject area. This site is well worth a visit.

The software does not have the glitter of modern Windows programs, but the exercises are student-oriented and several are unusually clever; they will intrigue and motivate the intro psych student. In the guilt detection task, for example, students find themselves guilty of a believable crime involving the theft of a purse from a college office and then are asked to take a word association test, which they think they can beat. The results may surprise them because of the way the data are collected. The program debriefs after each experiment, asking students to identify flaws in the design or ways to modify the experimental procedures. An instructor's manual is available.

The Psychology Place
http://www.psychologyplace.com

The Psychology Place is a Web site designed to supplement introductory psychology courses, at either the high school or college level. It offers a wide range of resources for faculty and students, such as teaching tips, research news, animations and demonstrations, interactive exercises, and links to other Web sites. The Op-Ed section features brief interviews with many leading psychology researchers who replied to a query: "What is the question that you are asking yourself — the question that most fascinates you right now?" Various subscription options are available, including institution-wide purchase.

Psychology: The Active Learner CD-ROM
Jane Halonen, Marilyn Reedy, and Paul Smith
The McGraw-Hill Companies
1221 Avenue of the Americas
New York, NY 10020-1095
(800) 338-3987
http://www.mhhe.com

The CD-ROM for Windows or Macintosh computers offers interactive exercises and critical thinking problems primarily for the introductory psychology course, covering all the core topics such as research methods, sensation and perception, consciousness, social psychology, and diversity. One exercise involves participating in a formal work group to improve the quality of the work environment.

Psychology Tutorials

http://psych.hanover.edu/Krantz/tutor.html

John H. Krantz of Hanover College offers students access to a number of very intriguing tutorials written by many people to help with their study of psychology. Examples include *Auditory Perception* by Norma Welch of McGill University, *Basic Neural Functioning* by John Krantz, *How We Perceive Sound* by the Franklin Science Museum, and the *Illusions Gallery* contributed by David Landrigan of University of Massachusetts, Lowell. The collection of tutorials for sensation and perception is the highlight of this site, though tutorials in other areas are starting to appear. Some of the tutorials require advanced browser capabilities.

Psychology with Style

http://www.uwsp.edu/acad/psych/apa4b. htm

Dr. Mark Plonsky of the University of Wisconsin, Stevens Point, makes excellent use of the Web with this online guide to writing APA-style research reports. The site contains general style information, examples, and specific advice about how to organize a report and how to present data, all based on the *APA Style Manual.*
Dr. Plonsky includes links to instructor notes and to other sites of interest.

PsychSim & PsychQuest

Thomas E. Ludwig
Worth Publishers
College Division
345 Park Avenue South
New York, NY 10010
(800) 446-8923
http://www.worthpublishers.com
facultyservices@sasmp.com

PsychSim, available for under $20 in Windows and Macintosh formats, provides computer-based tutorials in 16 subject areas of general psychology especially suited to the introductory psychology course. Topics include neural messages, classical conditioning, maze learning, iconic memory, visual illusions, social decision making, cognitive development, and others. Some of the tutorials include simulations and games to help psychology students understand and experience fundamental psychological principles, such as the characteristics of iconic memory as demonstrated by the classic Sperling experiments. (Be warned that this simulation may run too fast on modern processors and, thus, result in strange data.) Other simulations explore the variables affecting social decision making, the learning curves in maze experiments, and the power of two-dimensional cues used in judging aspects of visual space, as demonstrated by the Poggendorf and Ponzo illusions. The package comes with a brief student workbook, and the publisher provides the programs free or at reduced cost to faculty who adopt their texts for classes.

Also available from Ludwig is a CD-ROM called PsychQuest, which is similar to PsychSim in that it contains experiments, simulations, and self-quizzes, but its topics are specifically designed to answer real-life questions such as "How do we control how much we eat?" "Why do we feel depressed?" and "How do athletes use perceptual cues?" There are eight modules built around such questions. Also available on the CD-ROM are links to the Web for further resources.

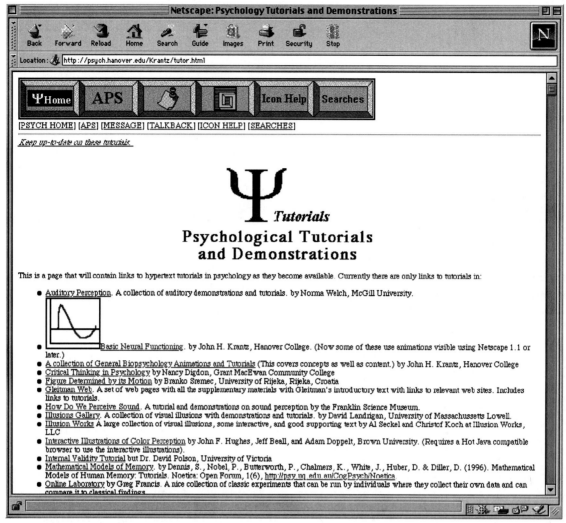

Location: http://psych.hanover.edu/Krantz/tutor.html

[PSYCH HOME] [APS] [MESSAGE] [TALKBACK] [ICON HELP] [SEARCHES]

Keep up-to-date on these tutorials

Ψ Tutorials
Psychological Tutorials and Demonstrations

This is a page that will contain links to hypertext tutorials in psychology as they become available. Currently there are only links to tutorials in:

- Auditory Perception. A collection of auditory demonstrations and tutorials. by Norma Welch, McGill University.

- Basic Neural Functioning. by John H. Krantz, Hanover College. (Now some of these use animations visible using Netscape 1.1 or later.)
- A collection of General Biopsychology Animations and Tutorials (This covers concepts as well as content.) by John H. Krantz, Hanover College
- Critical Thinking in Psychology by Nancy Digdon, Grant MacEwan Community College
- Figure Determined by its Motion by Branko Sremec, University of Rijeka, Rijeka, Croatia
- Gleitman Web. A set of web pages with all the supplementary materials with Gleitman's introductory text with links to relevant web sites. Includes links to tutorials.
- How Do We Perceive Sound. A tutorial and demonstrations on sound perception by the Franklin Science Museum.
- Illusions Gallery. A collection of visual illusions with demonstrations and tutorials. by David Landrigan, University of Massachussetts Lowell.
- Illusion Works A large collection of visual illusions, some interactive, and good supporting text by Al Seckel and Christof Koch at Illusion Works, LLC
- Interactive Illustrations of Color Perception by John F. Hughes, Jeff Beall, and Adam Doppelt, Brown University. (Requires a Hot Java compatible browser to use the interactive illustrations).
- Internal Validity Tutorial but Dr. David Polson, University of Victoria
- Mathematical Models of Memory. by Dennis, S., Nobel, P., Butterworth, P., Chalmers, K., White, J., Huber, D. & Diller, D. (1996). Mathematical Models of Human Memory: Tutorials. Noetica: Open Forum, 1(6), http://psy.uq.edu.au/CogPsych/Noetica
- Online Laboratory by Greg Francis. A nice collection of classic experiments that can be run by individuals where they collect their own data and can compare it to classical findings.

Psychology Tutorials and Demonstrations (http://psych.hanover.edu/Krantz/tutor.html). Reprinted by permission.

PsychWatch
http://www.psychwatch.com

Two graduate students working on their dissertation proposals launched this ambitious site to help people in psychology and psychiatry stay in touch with related Internet resources and media news events. They have put considerable effort into this, and the initiative includes a free electronic newsletter called Top-Ten, to which you can subscribe via e-mail. The newsletter highlights Web sites, upcoming events, and online articles about psychological topics, and the links embedded in the newsletter take you right to the resources.

Psych Web by Russ Dewey
http://www.psych-web.com

Russell Dewey of the Psychology Department at Georgia Southern University created and maintains this megasite of psychology resources for students and teachers of psychology, and hyperlinks to it exist on many of the other psychology-related lists. The site offers a collection of very helpful tip sheets for psychology students, some written for students at Georgia Southern and others contributed by faculty at different universities. Examples include an APA style crib sheet, advice on careers and applying to graduate programs, books on employment for psychology majors, tips on writing a psychology research paper, and suggestions to graduate students in search of an advisor. He also added self-quizzes that cover the basics of most introductory psychology courses, as well as a few advanced courses. Another service is called "discussion pages," where students can hold group discussions about psychology-related topics. Michael Nielson, also in the Psychology Department at Georgia Southern University, created and maintains a special section on the psychology of religion, and Dewey hopes to add more specialty items like this. Lists of links to other sites, including a comprehensive list of journals, abound on Psych Web. On the front page of the site, Russ Dewey says, "Write anytime. I enjoy e-mail."

PsycLink Software Information Service
http://plaid.hawk.plattsburgh.edu/psyclink/index.shtml

Peter Hornby, a psychology professor at SUNY Plattsburgh, developed this comprehensive software and Web resource site for people involved in the teaching, research, and practice of psychology. The site features links to related Web sites and a forum for opinions, but its main purpose is to provide access to information about software for all fields of psychology. If a program is not downloadable, then ordering information is given. The site is not fancy, but it offers a great deal of useful information.

The Random Thoughts of Louis Schmier
http://www.halcyon.com/arborhts/louis.html

Louis Schmier, a history professor at Valdosta State University in Georgia, maintains a voluminous collection of his essays about teaching, psychology, and student development. Teachers and others interested in educational psychology may want to explore this collection. Schmier is a frequent participant (and chronic cross-poster!) on mailing lists such as TIPS, OBTS-L, and other discussion forums targeted to teachers, contributing his "random thoughts" and inviting response. His postings are often quite long.

Recommended Popular Books on Psychology

by Charles G. Morris

http://www-personal.umich.edu/
~tmorris/goodbook.html

Tony Morris of the University of Michigan has compiled a thoughtful, 20-page annotated list of engaging and readable books, mostly paperbacks, especially suitable for psychology students. They range from Diane Ackerman's *A Natural History of Love* to Philip Zimbardo's 1977 classic on shyness. The list is widely recommended by psychology teachers as an excellent source of materials for outside reading. It can be downloaded from the Web site.

Search by Video

http://www.searchbyvideo.com/

This site is a clearinghouse for college recruitment videos and contains a database of more than 400 videos created by colleges, universities, and boarding schools to help students make an appropriate choice. The site was developed by Shelly Spiegel, who became frustrated and confused while helping her younger brother find the right college.

Shrink in a Box

http://www.dreamwv.com/shrink/shrink.
html

"Please take a seat.... The doctor will be with you shortly." This opening of this site suggests it is similar to Eliza, but this shrink works a lot more quickly – just four clicks to a diagnosis. Caroline McKeldin tried it out, deciding that her problem was with her cat. She was asked to choose how she felt: angry, sad, jealous, afraid, hateful, depressed. She selected "jealous." She was then asked to elaborate on these feelings, using a convenient "feelings pick 'n' click box." She picked "More Sedate." Other options were "Less Wistful" and "More Enraged." Next, she had to say who had made her feel this way, and was offered the choice among mother, father, man, woman, self, God, and animal. She chose "animal," of course. Finally, there came the requisite question about relationship with mother – this answer required a fill-in-the-blank. She said "good," just to be arbitrary (yet truthful). Here's her diagnosis: "Of this I am sure. Your jealousy [sic] overprotective subconscious has been wounded by your repressed animalistic Oedipal impulses." After that screenful, the Shrink in a Box had the decency to ask if she wanted a second opinion. Naturally, she clicked OK. And the response: "As I suspected – your unconscious mind refuses to facilitate your actualized attention-deficit disorder." Whatever.

Society for the Teaching of Psychology: Division Two, American Psychological Association

http://spsp.clarion.edu/mm/Division2/
d2.html

Division Two supports psychologists in academic institutions from secondary through graduate level and promotes excellence in teaching. Its Web site includes announcements of conferences on teaching, links to databases posting academic position vacancies, directories of members, and links to other resources on the Internet sorted by topical areas such as general psychology, history of psychology, clinical psychology, and behavior analysis.

StudentCenter

http://StudentCenter.com/

This site offers career-related information for students, including data about thousands of companies,

TIPS and the TIPSTERS

Anyone who teaches psychology, and anyone who likes to eavesdrop at the psychology faculty lounge, should know about the mailing list Teaching in the Psychological Sciences (TIPS). It was started by Bill Southerly of Frostburg State University in Maryland, whose doctorate from Purdue University is in child development and family studies. He has been fascinated by the potential of the Internet from the beginning. He had been actively participating on other mailing lists when it occurred to him that a group dedicated solely to the teaching of psychology would probably attract a large audience, particularly because it might help sustain that "professional high" psychology teachers feel after attending teaching-oriented sessions at professional meetings. From the beginning, he wanted to establish an environment in which people could comfortably disagree with one another without flaming, but in the early months he had to take a strong stance, because several participants just couldn't resist the temptation to express their own viewpoints by firing insults at others. Like many other mailing list moderators, Bill was accused of violating free speech when he exercised his moderator role, but he stood his ground and insisted that the mailing list maintain a professional tone. "Just as I wouldn't tolerate students in my class calling each other names when they disagree about a topic of discussion, I expect nothing less of my colleagues on TIPS." The mature TIPS rarely sees any flames, thanks to the way Bill set the tone.

The kinds of topics discussed on TIPS are many and varied. A recent, very lively one involved the procedures faculty use when they hand back tests, and how the method can result in negative reactions among some students. In another thread, participants actively discussed the forms of address that students and professors use in their psychology classrooms, and the impact this can have on the class environment.

Bill Southerly spends over an hour a day on TIPS-related issues, and his role in the group has shifted from active moderator to facilitator and technical consultant. He still reads every message, and he's there if you need him, though he is no "tekkie."

---

demographic data by state in the United States, and hints on resume preparation.

The Student Market
http://www.studentmkt.com/

Oren Milgram of San Jose State University decided the price of used textbooks would benefit from the Internet's economic scale, and if students could organize and communicate, they could exchange used textbooks without the overhead of retail bookstores. The WWW was an obvious place for such an activity, so he designed a Web-based store for used textbooks, searchable by keyword, which attracted thousands of visitors in its first few months. You can register at this site to post your own books for sale or find books that you need for the upcoming semester. The site does not actually sell books, but it puts students with books to sell in contact with those who want to buy, mostly via e-mail. You make your own exchange arrangements.

Study Tips on the 'Net
http://ouacinfo.ouac.on.ca/osca/study-tips.htm

There are many guides aimed at students to help them improve study skills and work habits, and this site, sponsored by the Ontario School Counsellors' Association, has links to many of them. Some guides are specific to one skill such as test-taking, but most present a full complement of strategies for improving all study skills from effective note-taking to time management to cramming.

Teachers of Psychology in the Secondary Schools
The TOPSS Web Page
http://spsp.clarion.edu/mm/topss/topss.htm
The TOPSS home page features teaching and curriculum resources, links to other related sites, and the e-mail directory created through the PsycList project started in 1993 to facilitate networking of people interested in teaching psychology at the high school level. The site has considerable information and support for psychology clubs, including ideas for projects.

TIPS
Main TIPS:
http://spsp.clarion.edu/Division2/d2.html
OTRP: http://www.lemoyne.edu/OTRP/

Send e-mail to
LISTSERV@FRE.FSU.UMD.EDU
Put in the body of the message:
SUBSCRIBE TIPS Yourname
TIPS stands for "Teaching in the Psychological Sciences," and this is an important resource for teachers of psychology. It is also a draw for students who like to listen in on the conversations of professors. Managed by Bill Southerly of Frostburg State University, the very large group discusses textbooks, resources, classroom strategies, theories in psychology, upcoming conferences, and many other subjects of interest to teachers of psychology.

In addition to its mailing list, TIPS also sponsors two Web sites. The general TIPS site describes the organization and provides links to membership enrollment, conference information, and relevant

news briefs, as well as to related psychology links.

TIPS maintains the OTRP (Office of Teaching Resources in Psychology), which develops and distributes teaching and advising materials as a service to Division 2 of the APA. The OTPR site provides full-text access to the TIPS journal *Teaching of Psychology* [October 1974 to present], links to member services, and a Teaching Resources section, with articles on anything from course syllabi to ethical issues. (See the entry for Office of Teaching Resources in Psychology.)

UG-PSYCHLIST
Send e-mail to
UG-PSYCHLIST-REQUEST@PSY.UQ.OZ.AU
Put in the body of the message:
SUBSCRIBE
The discussion forum is for undergraduate students whose major or minor is psychology, and topics include graduate school issues, undergraduate research, career options, internships, and anything else psychology undergrads like to discuss.

U.S. News and World Report: America's Best Graduate Schools
http://www.usnews.com/usnews/edu/beyond/gradrank/gpsych.htm
USNWR ranks the graduate schools in psychology at this Web site, including rankings for overall quality and by specialty. The site includes a description of how the rankings are determined and shows the point scores for each institution. Only U.S. institutions are included.

5 Psychology Resources by Discipline

The resources related to specific subject areas in psychology run the gamut from the humanistic JungWeb to the very specialized neuroscience site containing a detailed atlas of the human brain (The Whole Brain Atlas). They are not evenly balanced, and you'll find far more resources in some disciplines than others. In some ways, this is because psychologists in certain disciplines became comfortable with technological tools early and have had more time to create these resources. However, it also highlights the capabilities and limitations of computers. Neuroscientists, experimental psychologists, and statisticians, for example, find endless uses for computers because the machines do certain kinds of tasks so brilliantly. Nevertheless, a great many more resources have appeared since the first edition of *Psych Online*, and these new ones cover a remarkable range. This chapter groups the more specialized resources by discipline, with a section called "Other Resources" at the end for entries that don't fit easily into any of the other categories.

Biological Psychology and Neuroscience

Brain Science Resource Kit
http://www.cpl.uiuc.edu/~cholroyd/
brainsci/brainsci.html

Clay Holroyd, a graduate student in the Neuroscience Program at the University of Illinois at Urbana-Champaign, put up this Web page to provide links to a variety of newsgroups and Internet resources dealing with cognitive neuroscience. The page includes sections on job hunting, as well as links to various graduate departments with programs in the neurosciences.

Brainscape
brain.zip
by W. J. Wilson and I. a. ostergren
Available from ShrinkTank
(http://www.shrinktank.com/), the

neuroscience Web page at Indiana University (http://www.ipfw.edu/nf1/wilsonj/web/otherwww.htm), and other shareware repositories.

This DOS freeware is an amusing text-based adventure game to help students learn neuroanatomy. The game occurs inside the brain and players use anatomical terms (rostral, dorsal, etc.) to move about and pick up inventory items such as dopamine. (The second author seems to like lowercase letters.)

Cool Edit
Syntrillium Software
PO Box 60274
Phoenix, AZ 85082-0274
(602) 941-4327
syntrill@aol.com
http://www.syntrillium.com/cool.htm

Cool Edit is a digital sound editor for Windows that can be used to generate sound files that create a variety of auditory stimuli intended to stimulate

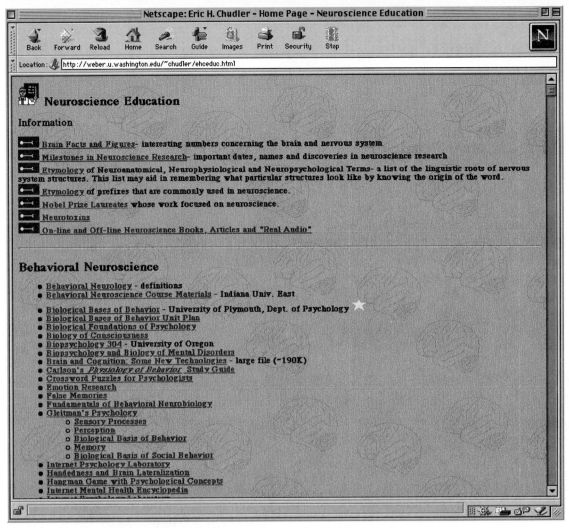

Eric Chudler's Neuroscience Education Resources.
(http://weber.u.washington.edu/~chudler/ehceduc.html). Reprinted by permission.

particular brain wave patterns such as alpha, beta, theta, or delta.

Its manual includes a complete guide to brain wave synchronization and the effects of various brain waves. To use this program, you'll need a minimum of 4 MB of RAM, 2 MB of free hard disk space, a sound card, speakers or headphones, and a mouse. You can combine sounds, create files designed to move you from one brain wave frequency to another, and even embed your own "subliminal" messages. Carefully constructed sound patterns like these have been used to induce sleep, improve alertness, enhance cognitive functioning, and treat various disorders, but research on actual benefits is not conclusive. The sounds are generally pleasing, though, particularly the ones that simulate waterfalls and

rivers. The full version of Cool Edit costs $50, and the "Lite" version is only $25.

Clinical Neurophysiology
CoolSpring Software
(301) 845-8719
CoolSpring@aol.com
http://users.aol.com/CoolSpring/
CSpring.html

CoolSpring publishes a variety of educational software (Windows and Macintosh) in the area of neuropsychology and medical neuroscience and some computer-based assessment tools. Products include *Clinical Neuropsychology*, *Neurological Illness*, and *Medical Labs*. You can view its catalog with descriptions of all its products at the Web site.

Dialog & News in Psychiatry and Psychobiology
sci.med.psychobiology

This unmoderated newsgroup has many discussions on psychoactive drugs, and some physicians and scientists participate. The group is informal, and topics might include an exchange about the marketing value of drug names or queries from people looking for drugs not available in the United States.

EEG Spectrum
http://www.eegspectrum.com

EEG Spectrum, Inc.
16100 Ventura Blvd., Suite 3
Encino, CA 91436-2505
(818) 788-2083

Sponsored by EEG Spectrum, Inc., this site provides resources on the use of EEG biofeedback. It features FAQs (frequently asked questions), descriptions of research on the use of the technique to treat disorders such as attention deficit disorder, bruxism (teeth grinding), brain injury, and post-traumatic stress disorder.

Eric Chudler's Neuroscience Education Resources
http://weber.u.washington.edu/~chudler/ehceduc.html

Eric Chudler is an assistant professor in the Department of Anesthesiology at the University of Washington in Seattle. The home page of his site focuses on systems neuroscience, but he has collected an exhaustive list of links to educational neuroscience resources (his degree is in psychology). Links are grouped into sections such as Brain Imaging/Brain Atlases, Sensory Systems, and Behavioral Neuroscience.

The Graphic Brain
Timothy J. Teyler
Brooks/Cole Publishing Company
511 Forest Lodge Rd.
Pacific Grove, CA 93950-5098
(800) 487-5510

The Graphic Brain uses computer-animated instruction to demonstrate what is otherwise difficult using static illustrations. This text-independent software includes 11modules (averaging 10-15 minutes each), which students can use to learn at their own pace, repeating difficult sections when necessary. Topics include neural network function, lateral inhibition, the movement of ions across the membrane, and transmitter binding/channel opening. This software can be run in both Windows and Macintosh computers.

Left/Right Brain Dominance Program
brainlr.zip
Ken Blystone
Available by download from ShrinkTank (http://www.shrinktank.com/) and other software repositories.

A small donation is requested to use this older shareware written in BASIC, which requires BASICA to run. The program asks 30 multiple choice questions to assess hemispheric specializations.

Neuro-Linguistic Programming
alt.psychology.nlp

The title may mislead you into thinking this is a scientifically oriented forum. Although some well-conceived contributions appear, the unmoderated newsgroup is usually home to a weird

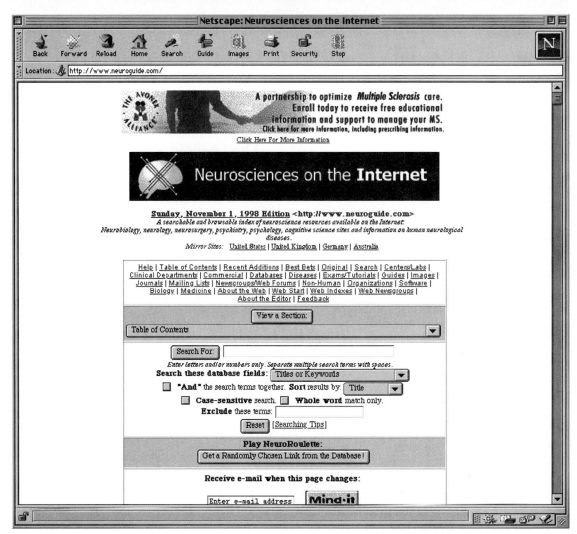

Neurosciences on the Internet (http://www.neuroguide.com). Reprinted by permission.

collection of postings on subjects such as conspiracies, alien abduction, subliminal perception, hypnosis, and the usual amount of sarcasm and flaming. It's an alt group, after all.

NEUROPSYCH

Send e-mail to neuropsych-request@mailbase.ac.uk and ask to be added to the list. This list is not automated.

Tony Ward at the MRC Applied Psychology Unit in Cambridge has initiated this list as an open forum for discussion on any topic relating to neuropsychology. Members help each other with all kinds of information from teaching resources to evaluation software.

Neuropsychology Central

http://www.premier.net/~cogito/neuropsy.html

This is a comprehensive site covering everything from assessment (tests, literature) to branches of neuropsychology (e.g., developmental, cognitive), to forums for discussion (mailing lists, bulletin boards), to home pages for specific laboratories and neuropsychologists. There are many sections to explore, each being of considerable depth.

Neurosciences on the Internet
http://www.neuroguide.com

Neil A. Busis has created a Web site for the neurosciences that has considerable depth and some very impressive search tools. If you start at the table of contents, you can see the large range of materials and links that is included on this site, organized into logical groupings to make subjects easier to find. However, if you like to take potluck, you can play "neuroroulette" and have a site chosen for you at random. The site publishes original articles from authors, which can include multimedia materials such as movies and sound files.

Neurosim
Biosoft
PO Box 10938
Ferguson, MO 63135
(314) 524-8029
or
37 Cambridge Place
Cambridge, CB2 1NS, UK
+44 (0) 1223-368622
http://www.biosoft.com

Neurosim is a set of interactive computer programs for DOS or Windows useful for teaching principles of neuronal activity and neural physiology. For example, the HH program simulates the Hodgkin-Huxley model of a neural impulse; the user can apply various drugs or alter ionic concentrations and temperature and then note the effects on the resulting neural conduction in a graphical printout. An animated cartoon shows the movement of molecules across the cell membrane. Other programs simulate circuits of neurons and the kinetic properties of single ion channels. The package is $399.

PharmInfoNet
http://pharminfo.com/

The Pharmaceutical Information Network site has a tremendous amount of information about pharmaceuticals, including a variety of publications, a database on drugs, job postings, and links to other pharmaceutical sites. The database on drugs is particularly impressive, and you'll be able to find most of the drugs used to treat behavioral disorders. Each entry includes side effects, major uses, research, and links to related information about the drug.

ProComp+
Thought Technology Ltd.
2180 Belgrave Avenue
Montreal, (Qc) Canada H4A 2L8
(800) 361-3651
http://www.thoughttechnology.com

Thought Technology provides a range of software and hardware products for computerized physiological monitoring used in research, assessment, and therapy. ProComp+ includes an encoder and computer interface, along with software to display and analyze the incoming data. The system accepts inputs from eight sensors of EMG, heart rate, skin conductance, and other physiological variables. Other products include portable stress control devices (GSR), myogram monitoring systems, and an advanced version of ProComp+ with additional capabilities.

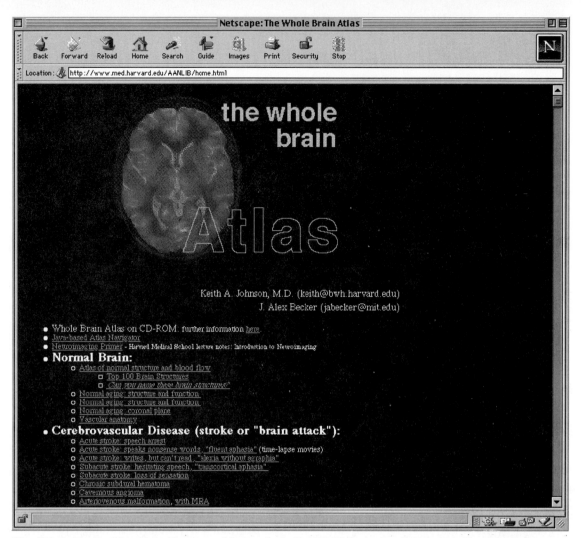

Location: http://www.med.harvard.edu/AANLIB/home.html

the whole
brain

Atlas

Keith A. Johnson, M.D. (keith@bwh.harvard.edu)
J. Alex Becker (jabecker@mit.edu)

- Whole Brain Atlas on CD-ROM: further information here.
- Java-based Atlas Navigator
- Neuroimaging Primer - Harvard Medical School lecture notes: Introduction to Neuroimaging
- **Normal Brain:**
  - Atlas of normal structure and blood flow
    - Top 100 Brain Structures
    - *Can you name these brain structures?*
  - Normal aging: structure and function
  - Normal aging: structure and function
  - Normal aging: coronal plane
  - Vascular anatomy
- **Cerebrovascular Disease (stroke or "brain attack"):**
  - Acute stroke: speech arrest
  - Acute stroke: speaks nonsense words, "fluent aphasia" (time-lapse movies)
  - Acute stroke: writes, but can't read, "alexia without agraphia"
  - Subacute stroke: hesitating speech, "transcortical aphasia"
  - Subacute stroke: loss of sensation
  - Chronic subdural hematoma
  - Cavernous angioma
  - Arteriovenous malformation, with MRA

The Whole Brain Atlas (http://www.med.harvard.edu/AANLIB/home.html) Reprinted by permission.

Research Issues in the Neurosciences
bionet.neuroscience

This active newsgroup discusses a wide range of issues in neuroscience from the hippocampus and amygdala to the role of drugs in behavior. Participants are an assortment of those interested in psychology, medicine, pharmacology, and other fields. A few cranks who like to discuss vague emissions emanating from the brain in the form of radio waves participate occasionally. They are promptly directed to more appropriate newsgroups.

Washington University Comprehensive Epilepsy Program
http://www.neuro.wustl.edu/epilepsy/

This site at Washington University in St. Louis offers a variety of resources for those interested in epilepsy, including bibliographies, discussion groups, and links to many other sites that describe current research in the area. The page includes a means for readers to add to the lists of links and resources, which should help keep it up-to-date.

The Whole Brain Atlas
http://www.med.harvard.edu/AANLIB/
home.html

The remarkable achievement developed by Harvard's medical school is an atlas that includes an enormous number of images of the central nervous system. The Web site offers extensive navigational controls so the visitor can click on brain areas to retrieve specific views and slices and read captions explaining the details of the image. The site includes images of normal brains as well as those with various disorders, such as Alzheimer's disease, Huntington's disease, and stroke. Some movies that display time-lapsed images are also available. The atlas is also available on CD-ROM with the same interface as the Web site and with 13,000 images.

Sensation and Perception

B-EYE
http://cvs2.anu.edu.au/andy/beye/
beyehome.html

Andrew Giger, a neuroscientist who works on vision in bees, created this intriguing site to illustrate properties of the bee's eye. Particularly appropriate for students studying sensation and perception, the site provides a description of how the bee's eye functions and a gallery of downloadable images that show what the world might look like to a bee. It also allows the visitor to set a few parameters (e.g., bee's position), run a program that simulates the optics of a honeybee, and display the resulting image.

Exploring Perception

Collin Ryan
Brooks/Cole Publishing Company
511 Forest Lodge Rd.
Pacific Grove, CA 93950-5098
(800) 487-5510

Exploring Perception allows instructors to demonstrate concepts in class and then assign interactions for students to try independently. The program includes five modules, each consisting of eight units, which in turn consist of six interactions. Topics covered include apparent movement, color perception, visual illusions, form perception, simultaneous color contrast, aftereffects, and sensory adaptation.

There is an instantaneous search and review feature which gives students feedback on their work.

IllusionWorks
http://www.illusionworks.com/

This site is the place to explore optical and sensory illusions, with its interactive demonstrations and puzzles, illusion artwork, and fully scientific explanations. The original site became so popular that it has split into an introductory site and an advanced site, the major difference being the level of scientific depth in the explanations.

Some of the illusions require Java and Shockwave plug-ins. It is also useful to have a powerful Web browser.

Internet Psychology Lab
http://kahuna.psych.uiuc.edu/ipl/

The Internet Psychology Lab (IPL) is an interactive group of demonstrations and experiments about visual and auditory perception, memory, learning, and cognition which requires end users to download and install several plug-ins. Once you have loaded the IPL plug-in, you can try the experiments such as Chimeric Faces, Reaction Time Tests, Stroop Effect, Tritone Paradox, and Ponzo Illusion. The goal of the Web site creators, from the University of Illinois, is to develop a multimedia, interactive psychology laboratory on the Web so that students can access it from dorms, labs, or homes.

Perception: A Computerized Approach

Life Science Associates
One Fenimore Road
Bayport, NY 11705-2115
(516) 472-2111
lifesciassoc@pipeline.com
http://www.pipeline.com/~lifesciassoc
Theodore Hirota of the University of Windsor in Canada developed this rich and detailed suite of DOS programs to teach and demonstrate perceptual topics such as the properties of energy, light, and color; the nature of the visual and auditory systems; and major theories and methodologies in sensation and perception (opponent process, trichromatic theory, signal detection theory, Gestalt organizing principles, etc.). The programs incorporate many graphics, animations, and experimental sessions placed into tutorial contexts, and they go well beyond the usual computer-based demos of perceptual phenomena. For example, the section on motion perception includes far more than a brief demonstration of the phi phenomenon. After the introduction, the sequence goes on to animate, explain, and allow users to experiment with many more advanced topics such as motion/velocity threshold, speed constancy, induced motion, motion aftereffects, multiple sequence effects, autokinetic effects, stroboscopic movement, and Korte's laws. The full package is $395, and individual modules can be purchased separately for $90 each. A subset of the modules is available as a student edition with lab manual for $29 for adoptions of 10 or more.

PLABDEMO

pdemo.zip
David J. Pittenger
Department of Psychology
Marietta College
Marietta, OH 45750
pittengd@marietta.edu
This DOS shareware offers a collection of visual experiments and demonstrations. Examples include afterimages, the cafe illusion, the Hermann grid, Mach bands, movement aftereffects, and color mixing. The user can adjust certain features on most of the demonstrations or experiments to assess how variables, such as color or saturation, influence the effects. For example, the afterimage demonstration allows the user to change the color of a large square that appears on the computer. Registration is $10.

SIRDSANI

Gareth Richards & Peter Chang
Platonic Software
17 Florence Avenue
Harehills
Leeds, LS9 7AL
United Kingdom
gareth@h1.ph.man.ac.uk
SIRDSANI stands for Single Image Random Dot Stereogram Animator, and it is a shareware program for DOS 286 or better computers with at least a VGA display. This program allows you to create stereograms and animate them on the computer screen to create some mesmerizing displays. The user can manipulate several features of the display, including the object embedded in the stereogram, variables affecting the angle of rotation, and the size of the object. You can print out the stereogram, though it will lose its animation, of course. The registered version is $10, and the demo is available from many ftp

sites with shareware repositories. A listing of several other programs that help you create stereograms is on the Web at SIRDS Programs Available (http://www-ai.ijs.si/sirds/).

VisionLab, pcSTEREOSCOPE and VisionWorks

Vision Research Graphics, Inc.
99A + Madbury Road
Durham, NH 03824
(603) 868-2090
http://www.vrg.com/
webmail@vrg.com

VisionLab and its companion hardware, pcSTEREOSCOPE, create a flexible laboratory environment for exploring visual phenomena. The hardware consists of goggles and a plug-in card that permit the PC to synchronize timing and display of stereoscopic images. The software includes demonstrations and experiments on topics such as visual illusions, word recognition, apparent motion, aftereffects, and random dot stereograms. The user can change the stimulus parameters of many of the demonstrations to view the effects of several visual variables.

VisionWorks is an advanced PC-based computer graphics system designed to be used by researchers as a visual stimulus generator and experiment controller, to create a standalone psychophysical experiment workstation. The base system can be augmented with several software and hardware options to increase the power of the workstation and add functionality. Examples include StimulusMaker (software for generating stimuli used in vision research), Neurophysiology Module (application programs to support rapid manipulation of stimuli and preconfigured stimuli sequences needed for single-unit recording applications), and Stereo Shutter Glasses and driver board (hardware add-ons for stereoscopic applications).

VScope and VSearch

MicroPsych Software
James T. Enns
UBC VSearch Lab
Department of Psychology
University of British Columbia
Vancouver, BC Canada V6T 1Z4
(604) 822-6634
www.interchange.ubc.ca/vsearch

James T. Enns has developed software programs for Macintosh computers that facilitate the design, construction, execution, and analysis of experiments on visual perception and visual search. VScope, a general purpose tachistoscope, enables researchers to import graphics to create displays and distracters and provides precise control over stimulus properties such as target complexity, location, timing, color, predisplay and postdisplay images, and onset and offset. The program collects subject responses in milliseconds. VSearch facilitates experiments on visual search using targets and distracters. The programs are $300 each.

SIRDS Programs Available

http://www-ai.ijs.si/sirds/SirdsSw.txt

The Jozef Stefan Institute in Ljubljana, Slovenia, offers a list of software programs that can be used to create single image random dot stereograms on the PC as part of its larger Web site on machine learning and artificial intelligence. The directory lists about 17 programs, most of which are freeware or shareware; each entry includes information on platform requirements, availability, and comments.

Social and Cross-Cultural Psychology

AGGRESS
**Send e-mail to
LISTSERV@MAELSTROM.STJOHNS.EDU
Put in the body of the message:
SUBSCRIBE AGGRESS Yourname**
  This mailing list is a forum for discussing all aspects of the psychology of aggression, including topics such as online "bullying."

American National Election Studies (ANES)
**User Support ICPSR
PO Box 1248
Ann Arbor, MI 48106
(734) 763-5010
www.icpsr.umich.edu**
  The CD-ROM ($65) for IBM-compatibles contains social science data collected over several decades on subjects such as affirmative action, arms control, civil rights, and gun control, as well as data on social, economic, and demographic characteristics of North Americans.

C-PSYCH
**Send e-mail to
LISTSERV@MAELSTROM.STJOHNS.EDU
Put in the body of the message:
SUBSCRIBE C-PSYCH Yourname**
  The C-PSYCH discussion group is open to all to discuss issues in cross-cultural psychology. Sunkyo Kwon at Humboldt University in Berlin, who is also the list owner for C-PSYCH's parent discussion group called TRANSCULTURAL-PSYCHOLOGY, started this group and facilitates the discussion. The group grew quickly and includes

many people from countries around the world.

Central Intelligence Agency
http://www.odci.gov/

**gopher://sunsite.unc.edu:70/7waissrc:/
ref.d/indexes.d/world-factbook.src**
  It may seem odd to place the CIA in this group, but this site maintains the *World Factbook*, which is a searchable resource for students interested in data about countries around the world. The *Handbook of International Economic Statistics* is also included.

The Census Bureau
http://www.census.gov/
  This is an enormous site with information about the census, future population trends, press releases, demographic programs, and statistical briefs. It also offers some downloadable statistics and software.

Coombsweb
http://coombs.anu.edu.au/
  The Australian National University maintains an extensive collection of social science materials accessible through the Web, gopher, ftp, and e-mail and provides links to many other related sites around the globe. This is a megasite with considerable depth and breadth, particularly in Asian-Pacific studies. The Coombspapers ANU Social Sciences Research Data Bank is accessible from the Web page or through anonymous ftp to coombs.anu.edu.au. Started in 1991 as an electronic repository of social science and humanities resources, Coombspapers includes a large variety of materials ranging from original research papers to extensive bibliographies. A great deal of

Netsite: http://www.icpsr.umich.edu/home.html

- ICPSR Home - Topical Archives -
contents - archive - summer - contacts - forums - sites

ICPSR
h • o • m • e • p • a • g • e

Welcome. The Inter-university Consortium for Political and Social Research (ICPSR), located within the Institute for Social Research at the University of Michigan, is a membership-based, not-for-profit organization serving member colleges and universities in the United States and abroad. ICPSR provides:

- Access to the world's largest archive of computerized social science data.
- Training facilities for the study of quantitative social analysis techniques.
- Resources for social scientists using advanced computer technologies.

***** **Table of Contents** *****

ICPSR: http://www.icpsr.umich.edu
website technical issues

Inter-university Consortium for Political and Social Research (http://www.icpsr.umich.edu/hom.html). Reprinted by permission.

material for those interested in cross-cultural psychology is located at this site.

Current Research in Social Psychology
http://www.uiowa.edu/~grpproc/crisp/crisp.html

This electronic journal, sponsored by the Center for the Study of Group Processes at the University of Iowa, began in 1995 and features peer reviewed articles in social psychology. Each issue (so far) has only one article, with titles such as "The Coalition Structure of the Four-Person Family" and "Assessing Fundamental Power Differences in Exchange Networks: Iterative GPI."

Cybermind
Send e-mail to
LISTSERV@LISTSERV.AOL.COM
Put in the body of the message:
SUBSCRIBE CYBERMIND Yourname

Cybermind is an unmoderated mailing list dedicated to discussing philosophy and psychology of cyberspace. Discussions have ranged from comparing the power of the Delete key on the computer keyboard to presidential power, to lurkers, to the boundaries of cyber-personalities. Activity is high, and the sense of community is strong – one member announced that his son was getting married that day and received many congratulatory responses.

ICPSR
http://www.icpsr.umich.edu/home.html

The Web site of the Inter-university Consortium for Political and Social Research (ICPSR) provides access to what is arguably the world's largest archive of social science data that can be downloaded and analyzed with statistical software. The range of datasets is awesome, including census data back to the 18th century, population statistics, attitude surveys, election results, public opinion data, social indicators, data on minorities and race relations, studies of decision making, and dozens of other areas. The site includes excellent navigation aids and useful assistance to help the researcher or student who wants to analyze these datasets to test new hypotheses or practice statistical analysis on live information rather than small, simulated datasets. Some datasets are also available on CD-ROM. The formats of the data vary and the visitor will need to be familiar with the Internet and with common statistical formats and coding schemes used by programs such as SAS and SPSS. Of course, previous researchers have rarely collected data in exactly the format you want. However, this site is a phenomenal achievement that continues to gather gargantuan quantities of data that were formerly collecting dust on magnetic tapes in inaccessible tape cabinets. ICPSR made it all available worldwide to new generations of researchers and will continue to add to this storehouse as new data are collected.

International Association for Cross-Cultural Psychology (IACCP)
http://www.fit.edu/CampusLife/clubs-org/iaccp/index.html

This site provides some basic information on the field of cross-cultural psychology and how to join the IACCP. The site offers conference information, books published by IACCP members, cross-cultural psychology graduate program information, and links to two publications associated with IACCP: *Journal of Cross-Cultural Psychology* and *Cross-Cultural Psychology Bulletin* – table of contents only. Recent article titles include "Individualist-Collectivist Tendencies in a Turkish Sample" and "Children's Attitudes Toward Physical Disability in Nepal: A Field Study."

Journal of Computer-Mediated Communication
http://jcmc.huji.ac.il/journal.html

This is a stellar example of an online journal, perhaps because its subject matter IS computers and communication. The graphics are simple but effective, back issues are clearly archived, and the search engine works with both keywords and concepts. Each issue is guest-edited and filled with topical articles. Examples of past issues are Collaborative Universities, Network and Netplay, and Designing Presence in Virtual Environments. In addition to articles, the site features a message board, calls for papers, and a site index. The permanent site editors are Margaret McLaughlin from the Annenberg School for Communication at University of Southern California and Sheizaf Rafaeli from the School of Business Administration at Hebrew University of Jerusalem.

The Keirsey Temperament Sorter
http://keirsey.com

This Web site is the official place to take the personality test called the Keirsey Temperament Sorter, based on the book *Please Understand Me* by David Keirsey and Marilyn Bates. The test uses the categories and types made famous by the Myers-Briggs Type Inventory, which include extroversion versus introversion, intuitive versus sensing, feeling versus thinking, and judging versus perceptive. The Web site provides detailed information about the personality types, as well as further information on Keirsey's books (*Please Understand Me II* is now out) and on how temperament affects everything from presidential leadership to marriage.

National Archive of Criminal Justice Data
http://www.icpsr.umich.edu/NACJD/home.html

The U.S. Department of Justice and the Inter-university Consortium for Political and Social Research cooperated to create this rich resource of crime-related data that can be downloaded for further analysis with statistical programs. The data come from a variety of sources such as polls by broadcast news programs (CBS News "48 Hours" Gun Poll; ABC/*Washington Post* Los Angeles Beating Poll), as well as government statistics on Supreme Court decisions, crime data, and confinement rates.

NETDYNAM
Send e-mail to
LISTSERV@MAELSTROM.STJOHNS.EDU
Put in the body of the message:
SUBSCRIBE NETDYNAM Yourname

The Network Group Dynamics Mailing List examines the social and psychological aspects of mailing lists and other online forums and the way that people participate in them. The very active group explores the dynamics of flame wars, impression formation online, the use of persuasion techniques, and other topics. One intriguing post listed the participants on NETDYNAM for a six-month period and calculated the "influence quotient" based on the number of times the individual posted a

message and the number of times each participant was referenced by another.

Psybersite at Miami University
http://miavx1.muohio.edu/~psybersite/

Miami University in Ohio sponsors this site of social psychology tutorials that have been written by advanced undergraduate and graduate psychology students. Titles include "The Psychology of Sports Fans: Why Your Favorite Team is 'Your' Team," "Optimistic Bias in Perceiving Physical and Mental Health Risks," and "How Real Is Computer-Mediated Communication?" Tutorials are well written and include hyperlinks to definitions of psychological terms and appropriate graphics. Many tutorials have self-quizzes at the end.

Psychology of Cyberspace
http://www1.rider.edu/~suler/psycyber/psycyber.html

John Suler, psychology professor at Rider University, has created this site dedicated to the emerging study of online behavior. He and his students have posted their essays, observations, and research results about the psychology of individuals, groups, and relationships in cyberspace, and they invite others to contribute as well. One major ongoing research project featured is about The Palace – an online environment where interaction is not just verbal but also graphical. Suler features an interview entitled "On Being a God" with Palace creator Jim Bumgardner.

Serendip
http://serendip.brynmawr.edu/

This site is difficult to categorize, but its basic philosophy is that "life's instructions are always ambiguous and incomplete." What you can expect from such a site is an eclectic mix of forums, articles, and scientific information about behavior, biology, and complex systems. It also features several interactive psychology-related games and simulations such as prisoner's dilemma. Many of the simulations require a Java-enabled browser.

soc.culture._____

USENET has a very large collection of newsgroups in the soc.culture hierarchy where the third level is either the name of the country or the cultural-ethnic group (e.g., Malagasy, Meghreb, Mexican, New Zealand, Taiwan, Tamil, Thai, Ukrainian, USA, Vietnamese, etc.). On many of them, participants contribute their postings in the native language (as best they can, using ASCII). Politics is a favorite subject, and America bashing is not uncommon on some of them. The groups often include people who are not citizens of the country itself but are interested in it for one reason or another. For example, some are planning to visit the country on vacation or apply to a university there. As usual, there is considerable cross posting, particularly for groups dealing with neighboring countries.

SOCPSY-L
**Send e-mail to
LISTSERV@UGA.CC.UGA.EDU
Put in the body of the message:
SUBSCRIBE SOCPSY-L Yourname**

Though not highly active, this list is still useful nonetheless for anyone interested in social psychology.

Social Psychology Network
http://www.wesleyan.edu/spn

The site was originally developed for Scott Plous's social psychology course at Wesleyan University but has grown to feature resources for a wider audience. Social psychology links include prejudice, negotiation, and persuasion. Helpful academic links highlight sources for funding, software, textbooks, and scholarly journals.

Trancenet.org
http://www.trancenet.org/

Trancenet is a weekly Web magazine "championing psychological freedoms in cults, corporations and family groups," and it features timely news articles as well as smaller "webzines" linked to its home page. There are webzines covering movements and organizations such as Heaven's Gate, The Way International, Hare Krishna, and Transcendental Meditation. Each 'zine has articles, FAQs, critiques, and research information. One, entitled *Shameless Mind*, is about the antics and work of Deepak Chopra, the prolific and now very rich proponent of quantum healing, ayurveda, and "spiritual success." The title of this 'zine is derived from his book *Ageless Body, Timeless Mind*. There are news stories about the Chopra phenomenon and plenty of critiques as well.

TRANSCULTURAL-PSYCHOLOGY
**Send e-mail to
LISTSERV@VM1.NODAK.EDU
Put in the body of the message:
SUBSCRIBE TRANSCULTURAL-PSYCHOLOGY Yourname**

This InterPsych discussion forum, led by Sunkyo Kwon at Humboldt University in Berlin, deals with cross-cultural psychology. Membership is worldwide, though the activity level is relatively low.

Social Decision-Making and Prisoner's Dilemma Simulations

Several social decision-making simulations are available for research purposes, demonstrations, class exercises, or just amusement. These programs follow a general format based on the prisoner's dilemma, an interpersonal game exploring decision making in situations in which the outcome of an individual's decision depends on what another person decides. Prisoner's dilemma and other computer-based social decision-making simulations rely heavily on formal game theory and mathematics, so they are well suited to a computerized simulation approach.

The prisoner's dilemma scenario involves two prisoners held by the police. The prisoners are separated, told the rules, and asked to decide whether to give evidence. Both prisoners are told that, if neither gives evidence, they both will be tried on a minor charge and probably receive a minimum jail sentence. If only one gives evidence, the snitch will go free but the other prisoner will receive the maximum penalty. If both give evidence, both will receive a moderate sentence. Each prisoner has to make decisions that result in different payoffs, depending on what the other prisoner decides to do. Research on this dilemma generally shows that most people tend to choose a competitive rather than a cooperative strategy, one that offers a chance at personal freedom, though the cost to the other prisoner might be high. Statistically, this strategy results in lower payoffs overall, but only a minority of people choose the more cooperative strategy that could pay off for both prisoners — that is, refusing to give evidence.

Another scenario is the trucking game, in which the subject attempts to drive a truck to its destination, either by taking a shorter route over a single-lane road or a longer route over a two-lane road. The payoffs depend on the combination of choices made by the player and the opponent. For example, the player will make the most money by choosing the single-lane road only if the opponent chooses the longer route. A variation allows the player to erect a gate so the opponent can't use the single-lane road at all.

Psychologists have used games like this to explore social dilemmas of all kinds in which interdependent decision making is involved. Will a diner choose the filet mignon rather than the chicken when the group has decided to share the check equally? Will a manager hoard information that should be shared with other managers if sharing might lead to advancement of the individual's colleagues?

Theoretically, these games assess the variables that underlie the complex choices people make about whether they should contribute to the common good or take a free ride on the sacrifices of others. By manipulating the number of people in the decision-making group, the number of times the group plays the game, and the various payoffs and penalties, researchers have learned a great deal about psychological strategizing. People in smaller groups tend to choose more cooperative strategies that maximize the common good, particularly if they know they will be working together for a long time.

Variations of social decision-making simulations can be found in MEL Lab, Psychology on a Disk, PsychSim, and strategy.zip, as well as at the Serendip Web site. A good introduction to the topic is found in Glance, N.S., & Huberman, B.A. (1994). The dynamics of social dilemmas. *Scientific American*, March, 76–81. The issue also includes the code to write your own game if you're familiar with BASIC.

Sherry Turkle
http://web.mit.edu/sturkle/www/
Sherry Turkle of MIT is an active researcher, writer, and speaker on the topic of computer culture, and her home Web site contains a summary of her book, *Life on the Screen: Identity in the Age of the Internet* (Simon and Schuster, 1995). The site also contains syllabi and resources for the courses she teaches, with intriguing titles such as *Gender, Technology, and Computer Culture* and *Psychology and Technology*.

United Nations
http://www.un.org

gopher://gopher.undp.org/
or gopher to: gopher.undp.org
The site contains texts of various UN resolutions, publications, and press releases and offers links to other United Nations gophers such as UNESCO.

The University of Virginia Social Sciences Data Center
http://www.lib.virginia.edu/socsci/
The Social Sciences Data Center provides an excellent means to obtain certain kinds of demographic and economic statistics that can be downloaded and entered into a statistics package for further analysis. The service allows the visitor to choose the population subset and the variables and choose the output method. For example, you could obtain personal income data by region, request that they be placed into the public ftp site, and then download the file to your statistics software. Some services are restricted only to UVA students and faculty because of licensing arrangements, but several are open to the public.

U.S. Information Agency
http://www.usia.gov/
The home page of USIA announces educational and cultural exchanges with other countries and offers a repository of information on U.S. history, economics, society, and culture.

Abnormal, Clinical, and Counseling Psychology

See chapter 6.

Cognition, Learning, and Memory

Altweb: Alternatives to Animal Testing on the Web
http://www.sph.jhu.edu/~altweb/
This site, sponsored by the Johns Hopkins School of Public Health's Center for Alternatives to Animal Testing, provides background information, monthly updates, and science and regulation news about alternatives to animal testing. Of particular interest is the Educational Resources section, which offers links to hundreds of online resources.

Altweb features journal abstracts from *ATLA, In Vitro Animal,* and *JAWS*, full-text technical reports from the center and a search engine.

ASK
Roger Shank
Department of Psychology
Northwestern University Institute for the Learning Sciences
(491) 847-3500
http://www.ils.nwu.edu

The Institute for the Learning Sciences (ILS) develops a variety of computer-based learning environments based on the principles of cognitive psychology, one of which is the ASK system. The ASK program capitalizes on people learning by doing, by failing, and by hearing stories of case histories. The technology incorporates video clips, and users can query the system to hear answers from the experts. It is being applied in a variety of learning settings such as the military, where videotaped interviews with experienced officers are made available to assist trainees in simulated battlefields, and in several health-related areas.

Behavior Analysis
http://www.coedu.usf.edu/behavior/behavior.html

The Behavior Analysis Web site at the University of South Florida collects relevant resources spanning the Internet, including mailing lists, electronic journal pointers, and an e-mail directory of people interested in behavior analysis. Of particular interest is the section on programmed instruction.

BEHAV-AN
Send e-mail to
LISTSERV@VM1.NODAK.EDU
Put in the body of the message:
SUBSCRIBE BEHAV-AN Yourname

The list discusses experimental and applied analysis of behavior, with a behavioristic bent. Moderated by Joseph Plaud of University of North Dakota, the list is designed to encourage communication about the theories and applications of behavioral analysis.

Cognitive Psychology Online Laboratory
http://www.psych.purdue.edu/~coglab/

This site gives you the chance to learn various principles of cognitive psychology by experiencing them in actual experiments right on the Web. To do so, you will need a browser that supports Java applets. Experiments are simple but powerful and are all fully explained. Titles of experiments include Mental Rotation, Visual Search Task, and Memory Span. The Psychology Department at Purdue University developed this site and welcomes users' comments and questions.

Creating Computer Programmed Instruction
Kale M. Kritch and Darrel E. Bostow
The Center for Programmed Instruction
Kritch@gte.net
http://www.tampatech.com/pi/

The package includes several tutorials on how to create computer programmed instruction, plus worksheets, exercises, and example programs. For instance, one group of tutorials explains how to use PC-CAI Tutor, an authoring language for developing programmed instruction. Some of the materials are also available for download.

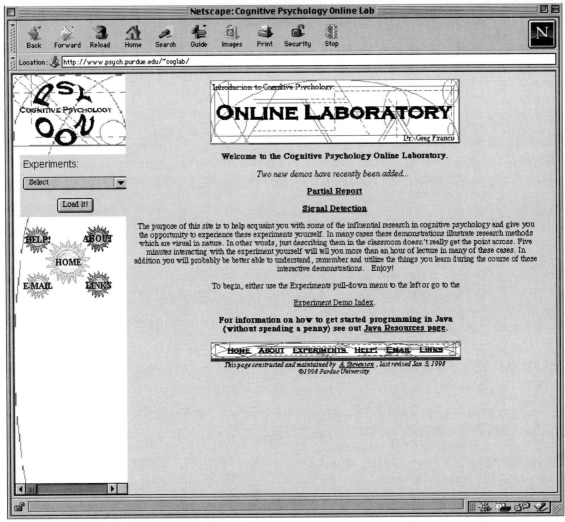

Cognitive Psychology Online Laboratory (http://www.psych.purdue.edu/~coglab). Reprinted by permission.

CyberRat
(800) 338-3987
http://www.mhhe.com/helpdesk/cyberrat/
contents.html

Roger Ray of Rollins College developed this CD-ROM for Windows and Macintosh platforms that creates a multimedia operant conditioning laboratory simulation. The program features a video presentation of a live rat whose realistic behavior and responsiveness to the rewards you deliver through the magazine are created by seamlessly linking short video segments from a database of 850 behavioral clips. You can use shaping to condition a wide variety of behaviors and observe the results of various reinforcement schedules. The program includes guidance for experimenters who choose their subjects from a colony room based on genetic learning characteristics and experimental histories. Experimental variables such as degree of deprivation, reinforcement magnitude, and schedules of reinforcement can be manipulated. The program ($278) also has extensive graphics and statistical capabilities for analyzing results. Not surprisingly, it is very resource intensive in terms of computer hardware.

DEVPSY

**Send e-mail to
LISTSERV@VM.Tulsa.cc.ok.us
Put in the body of the message:
SUBSCRIBE DEVPSY Yourname**

http://www.tulsa.oklahoma.net/~jnichols/
stulists.html

DEVPSY is a mailing list primarily for students enrolled in developmental psychology courses, but faculty are welcome to join as well. Discussion topics relate to child development, adolescence, and adult development. Specific topics have been about the advantages of early pregnancy detection tests, raising children with doubt and shame, and Skinner vs. Chomsky.

EARLI

**Send e-mail to
LISTSERV@NIC.SURFNET.NL
Put in the body of the message:
SUBSCRIBE EARLI Yourname**

The European Association for Research on Learning and Instruction (EARLI) sponsors this general list to promote discussion in the area of instructional and educational research. A special interest group sublist on assessment and evaluation issues is also available (EARLI-AE) at the same LISTSERV address.

Experiments in Cognitive Psychology

**Stanford University
Office of Technology Licensing
900 Welch Road, Suite 350
Palo Alto, CA 94304-1850
(650) 723-0651
http://www.stanford.edu/group/otl**

This program for Macintosh computers includes 21 experiments dealing with cognitive topics such as visual search, letter recognition, memory span, prose comprehension, perceptual

comparison, and fact retrieval. The experiments are generally based on classic research studies. The program can be licensed for a psychology laboratory for $400.

 ftp

Intuitive Inventory Management Software (IIMS)

**J. Meyer and M. Eben-Chaime
Ben-Gurion University
http://www.plattsburgh.edu/psyclink/
archive.shtml**

IIMS is an experimental DOS freeware program to study intuitive decision-making using inventory management as the content framework. The system simulates an inventory system in which seven items can be stocked and the demand, prices, costs, and supply constraints can be manipulated.

Laboratory in Classical Conditioning

**James O. Benedict
Little Professor Book Center
1790 East Market Street,
Harrisonburg, VA 22802
Phone: 540-574-0620
FAX: 540-434-6628**

This virtual laboratory (formerly distributed by Conduit) contains four simulations in classical conditioning in which students choose values for the independent variables and generate data based on their choices for analysis. In the salivary conditioning simulation, for example, students can manipulate the number of acquisition and extinction trials, the intensity of the conditioned stimulus (tone), the size of the unconditioned stimulus (food) UCS, and the duration and timing of the variables. Other classical conditioning simulations explore suppression ratio, blocking effect, and taste aversion. The DOS interface looks primitive compared with more modern conditioning simulations, but the program is easy to use.

Portrait of a Software Author

Pierre Mercier, psychology professor at the University of Ottawa, is an active researcher in the area of learning and cognition and is an enthusiastic advocate for the use of computers in psychology. He developed the Rescorla-Wagner Associative Simulator to verify theoretical predictions of learning models in his research, but as the project unfolded he saw the usefulness of the software for teaching as well. The graphical user interface makes it easier for students to learn its features quickly.

He generously contributed the software to the *Behavior Research, Methods, Instrumentation, and Computers* (BRMIC) library on COMPSYC, where it can be downloaded freely by psychology faculty and students and installed on IBM-compatible computers at will. By now, it's probably made its way into labs all over the world. Future plans include enhancements that will add additional models to test and a French version for teaching in Québec and Europe. He's also impatiently waiting for the Internet to support accents in a standardized way. For example, his own e-mail system allows him to enter é, but the e-mail systems of others, including my own, interpret the characters in amusing ways. Québec came out Quibec on my end. I sympathize with his frustration about Anglocentrism on computers and the Internet; when I was composing this paragraph, my very advanced and powerful word processor insisted "Québec" was misspelled and offered to replace it with "Quebec."

Laboratory in Cognition and Perception, v3
C. Michael Levy and Sarah E. Randsell
http://www.psychologysoftware.com/

This program has been upgraded for Windows and now offers 20 experimental areas for students to explore, using a demonstration mode, laboratory mode, and an advanced projects mode in which they can construct many variations on the theme presented in the module. Topics include signal detection, feature detection, spatial cognition, memory without awareness, reasoning from prose, and others. The program features an "intelligent" spreadsheet that helps students report data, even if they have never used a spreadsheet program before. Another program called Manuscript Mentor is included, which guides students through the process of writing an APA-style report. The program and the impressive 200-page *Student's Manual* can be purchased on the Web.

The Missouri Automated Reinforcer Assessment (MARA)
Madeleine Vetterott, Jayne Callier, & Matthew Hile
Available via download from CUSSN at http://www.uta.edu/cussn/diskcopy.htm in the Clinical/Therapeutic category.

This older DOS freeware program was developed to help identify reinforcers for individuals, using the expert system software Knowledge Pro. Users are asked a sequence of questions about what they like and don't like, and the program branches to more specific questions. Following the questions, the user selects his or her favorite items from lists sorted according to the responses on the earlier questions and by the type of reinforcer (edible reinforcers, social reinforcers, activities, tangible things, etc.). The output can be printed or saved to disk.

Noetica: A Cognitive Science Forum
http://psych.psy.uq.oz.au/CogPsych/
Noetica

Mirror site in the U.S.:
http://www.cs.indiana.edu/Noetica/

This electronic journal of the Australasian Cognitive Science Society is sponsored by the Department of Psychology at the University of Queensland in Australia. The second Web address is a mirror site at Indiana University that will have faster response times for North Americans.

Perception, Memory, Judgment & Reasoning
sci.cognitive

The unmoderated newsgroup is a forum for discussion of cognition and for exchanging information about research and instrumentation. Examples of relevant postings deal with the homunculus, cybernetic vision, computer models of reasoning, and software to create "mind-maps." Less relevant postings also appear, perhaps because of cross-postings, such as one dealing with human behavior during disasters. The newsgroup seems mercifully less populated with harsh exchanges than many others.

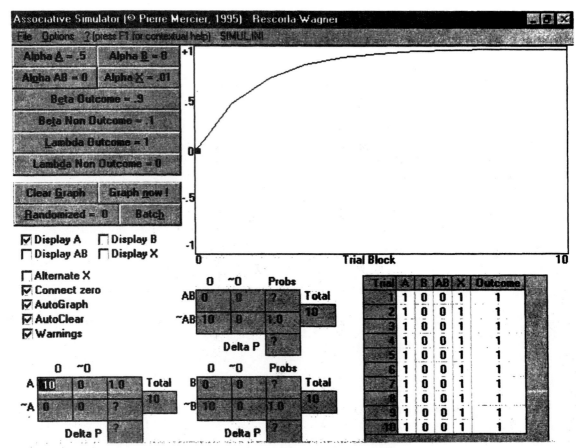

Rescorla Associative Simulator, by Pierre Mercier. Reprinted by permission.

 ftp

The Rescorla-Wagner Associative Simulator

rw.zip
Pierre Mercier
School of Psychology
University of Ottawa
Ottawa, Ontario CANADA
nitch@acadvw1.uottawa.ca
Download from:
http://www.plattsburgh.edu/psyclink/
archive.shtml

Pierre Mercier created this graphically vivid Windows program in Visual Basic to simulate the Rescorla-Wagner and Pearce-Hall models of learning. The software allows the user to change parameters of the conditioning situation and note the effects graphically.

The graphic user interface is quite impressive, and the program includes context-sensitive help.

Sniffy, the Virtual Rat
Jeff Graham, Tom Alloway, and
Lester Krames
Brooks/Cole Publishing Company
511 Forest Lodge Rd.
Pacific Grove, CA 93950-5098
(800) 487-5510

Sniffy is a software program (Windows or Macintosh) featuring a virtual rat used to teach the principles of operant conditioning, bypassing the expense and ethical constraints of a live rat lab for student experimentation. The rat lives in a virtual Skinner box and displays a range of behaviors such as scratching, licking, drinking, eating, and . . . sniffing. Students can train Sniffy by delivering food pellets into the hopper, and, because Sniffy has been programmed to behave more like a normal rat, the student must show great patience and careful timing to help Sniffy associate the sound of the food magazine with the food, and then use this sound as a secondary reinforcer to shape Sniffy's behavior. After training, the student can manipulate reinforcement schedules and observe the results. The program also includes some pretrained Sniffies for the impatient or for those with limited lab time.

Psychology of Consciousness

The Association for the Study of Dreams
http://www.asdreams.org/
ASD is "non-profit, international, multidisciplinary organization dedicated to the pure and applied investigation of dreams and dreaming." Its Web site offers an extensive collection of resources: sample articles from its journal called *Dreaming*, an online bookstore, conference information, news articles, and an active bulletin board. The site is searchable and clearly organized.

NSF Center for Biological Timing
http://cbt.virginia.edu
Maintained by the National Science Foundation, this site includes links to a variety of resources on biological clocks and sleep.

Pendulum Hypnosis
pendul.zip
http://bhs.broo.k12.wv.us/files/windows.htm
This shareware Windows software provides some information about self-hypnosis and a variety of animated images, including the pendulum, which might help you achieve the desired state. The registered version is $10 plus shipping and handling, and a demo is available by download from CompuServe.

The Sleep Well
http://www-leland.stanford.edu/~dement/
Dr. William C. Dement, director of the Stanford University Sleep Disorders Clinic, created this site dedicated to everything sleep-related. There are links to sleep disorders, sleep activism, journals, sleep-related humor, conferences, snoring, the quiz "How Sleepy Are You?" and advice on how to sleep better. It provides an excellent balance of information for professionals, students, and the general public.

Sleepy Bear Dream Interpretation Site
http://myenvoy.com/sleepybear/
Though the title seems frivolous, the site is an intriguing one that highlights people's fascination with dreams and dream analysis. The site includes descriptions of dreams, and visitors can view the reactions of other people and add comments of their own. Information about Jung's theories of dreams is ubiquitous, but where can you find out how real people have interpreted the dream "Donuts for All" (complete with a rainbow-sprinkled graphic)? Classic dream titles include "Yo Yo Ma," "Rental Car," "Accused!" and "Inept Hostess." All submissions and interpretations remain anonymous.

Parapsychology

Anomalous Cognition
http://info.psy.uva.nl/psychonomie/anomal.html

The Anomalous Cognition Web site in the Netherlands conducts online experiments on topics such as mind over matter and precognition. In one experiment, for example, the participant's goal is to "influence" a random number generator that is affecting the size of an animated rectangle so that the object will grow or shrink according to a prespecified goal. Some of the experiments require specialized plug-ins, such as Shockwave. The site also allows people to submit applications to run their own experimental series.

Cognitive Sciences Laboratory
http://www.lfr.org/csl/index.html

The mission of the government-sponsored Cognitive Sciences Laboratory is to determine which parapsychological phenomena can be validated scientifically, understand the underlying mechanisms, and explore practical applications. The Web site describes the lab's philosophical approach and explains the kinds of protocols that are used to explore parapsychological phenomena. The site also includes a useful glossary of terms.

Consciousness Research Laboratory
http://www.psiresearch.org

The Consciousness Research Laboratory at the University of Nevada, Las Vegas, focuses on scientific research on anomalies of human consciousness. The Web site describes some of the lab's research on mind-matter interactions and provides an extensive FAQ on psi, as well as links to additional information on psi.

The FAQ was developed by an interdisciplinary group of scientists and scholars interested in parapsychology. It is comprehensive and covers major research approaches, and examples of experiments in parapsychology; criticisms and methodological problems; a brief history of parapsychological research; and information about popular phenomena such as ghosts, poltergeists, channeling, and psychokinesis.

Koestler Parapsychology Unit
http://moebius.psy.ed.ac.uk/kpu.html

The Koestler Parapsychology Unit is housed in the Department of Psychology at the University of Edinburgh, and its Web site is a well-done resource. It includes reading lists, research methods, and extensive discussions of some of its research areas. One is the ganzfield ESP phenomenon, in which senders attempt to transmit mental images of videoclips they are viewing to passive recipients. Another involves investigation of DMILS, the acronym for direct mental interaction with living systems. This research area includes studies of "remote staring," a laboratory analog of the common feeling that someone is staring at you. The site also includes online experiments for visitors.

Princeton Engineering Anomalies Research
http://www.princeton.edu/~pear/

Housed within the Human Information Processing Group at Princeton University, this research program scientifically explores the interaction of human consciousness with sensitive physical devices, systems, and processes. Experiments are conducted in which human operators attempt to influence the behavior of various kinds of machinery through volition. The information on the Web site stresses the role of human consciousness as an active agent in physical reality, and the site contains essays on potential technological applications and cultural implications.

The RetroPsychoKinesis Project
http://www.fourmilab.ch/rpkp

The RPK project explores the hypothesis that people can influence random events (such as dice throws, coin tosses, and random number generators). The experiments can be conducted online, and results are posted. The site includes abstracts of related research papers, interviews with professionals, and various other links of interest.

Rhine Research Center
http://www.rhine.org

The Rhine Research Center, located adjacent to the Duke University campus, is a nonprofit research organization that uses the scientific method to explore parapsychological phenomena. The Web site includes a history of the center, abstracts from recent issues of the *Journal for Parapsychology*, descriptions of study opportunities, and links to related sites.

The Skeptic's Dictionary
http://www.dcn.davis.ca.us/˜btcarrol/skeptic/dictcont.html

The Skeptic's Dictionary was created by Robert T. Carrol, a philosophy teacher at Sacramento City College in California. In the introduction, he warns readers that he is not trying to present a balanced account of paranormal research or literature. His dictionary is "a Davidian counter-balance to the Goliath of occult literature." His extensive entry

for parapsychology maintains that the research is characterized by incompetence, deception, and fraud.

Life Span Development

ALZHEIMER
Send e-mail to majordomo@wubios.wustl.edu Put in the body of the message: SUBSCRIBE ALZHEIMER

http://www.biostat.wustl.edu/ALZHEIMER/

People suffering from Alzheimer's disease and their caregivers can find support and encouragement through this mailing list. Discussions include policies, treatments, caregiving issues, and research on the disorder. When you subscribe, you'll be asked to fill out a survey so the list owners can learn more about the nature of your interest. The list is sponsored by the Alzheimer Disease Research Center at WashingtonUniversity in St. Louis, Missouri, which also maintains an Alzheimer-related Web site for researchers and patients.

Alzheimer Web Home Page
http://dsmallpc2.path.unimelb.edu.au/ad.html

This Australian site, maintained by David Small at the University of Melbourne, provides information and resources to researchers working on Alzheimer's disease, a progressive disorder of the brain that causes memory loss, confusion, and personality changes. It provides brief updates on recent research, bibliographies, lists of conferences, and information about associations and support groups

The World of the Paranormal

The Internet is a magnet for people who want to relate their psychic experiences, discuss the latest evidence for alien abductions, and offer their insights about crop circles. Many of these forums can be wild and woolly places, and flaming is not unusual. The sarcasm level from skeptics who participate sometimes gets high. For example, in response to a post about psychic communication with animals, one fellow suggested that the poster put his cat on a world map on the floor and then tell it about all the cans of tuna it would get if it would find oil using its psychic powers. Another suggested that an ax might offer additional motivation to encourage the cat to perform. Almost every message is cross-posted to many other groups. The following are some examples of the newsgroups:

alt.alien.visitors
alt.astrology
alt.paranet.science
alt.paranet.ufo
alt.ufo.reports

alt.alien.research
alt.paranet.paranormal
alt.paranet.skeptic
alt.paranormal
sci.skeptic

The mailing list called the Parapsychology Discussion Forum (PSI-L) is a kinder and gentler forum for the discussion of unusual psychological phenomena. To subscribe, send e-mail to LISTSERV@VM.ITS.RPI.EDU with SUBSCRIBE PSI-L Yourname in the body of the message.

More academic information about parapsychology, including university departments that do research in the area, are listed under the Parapsychology heading in this chapter.

The American Academy of Child and Adolescent Psychiatry Homepage
http://www.Aacap.org/web/aacap

AACAP's home page keeps members informed of events in research, legislation, government affairs, continuing education, and upcoming conferences, and it provides catalogs of its publications and the AACAP directory. The site features *Facts for Families*, AACAP's fact sheets for children and their families on a variety of topics, which are available in English, Spanish, and French.

ANXIETY-DEPRESSION-YOUTH
See YANX-DEP in this section.

This discussion group has moved to a new host and changed its name to YANX-DEP.

Child Abuse and Neglect CD-ROM
National Clearinghouse on Child Abuse & Neglect Information
330 C Street, SW
Washington, DC 20447
(800) 394-3366

This software for IBM-compatibles contains a database of more than 18,000 bibliographic citations and abstracts of literature dealing with child abuse and neglect. Also included are databases covering legal issues, relevant organizations, and public awareness materials. The disk is available to institutions that send a letter on official letterhead, expressing an interest in the product.

CHILDES (Child Language Data Exchange System)
http://poppy.psy.cmu.edu/

CHILDES is a set of software programs and computational tools to facilitate the analysis of child language transcripts and automate the process. This Web site includes the full text of the manual, access to the CHILDES database, a Web-based conference to promote discussion of the software programs and the research area, and information about how to obtain the software and become a member of the CHILDES project.

Children Youth Family Education Research Network
http://www.cyfernet.org

This Web site features "practical, research-based" information on family and child-related matters. There are sections on current events/conferences, research, and resources, covering everything from   statistics and demographics to online activities for children and youth.

PIAGET-LIST
Send e-mail to
MAJORDOMO@UNIXG.UBC.CA
Put in the body of the message:
SUBSCRIBE PIAGET-LIST

This lower-volume, unmoderated mailing list supports members and nonmembers of the Jean Piaget Society to provide a forum for discussing developmental research and applications.

The Jean Piaget Society (JPS)
http://www.piaget.org

Founded in 1970, the society includes scholars, teachers, and researchers interested in the study of knowledge and development. The site highlights upcoming conferences and provides the online version of *The Genetic Epistemologist*, the journal of the Jean Piaget Society. Directions for subscribing to its mailing list (PIAGET-LIST) are included.

Social Security Online
http://www.ssa.gov/SSA_Home.html

This U.S. government site has numerous resources on social security benefits and a large volume of downloadable demographic statistics under the Research and Data section.

YANX-DEP
Send e-mail to
LISTSERV@MAELSTROM.STJOHNS.EDU
Put in the body of the message:
SUBSCRIBE YANX-DEP Yourname

This open LISTSERV discussion group, led by Phil Endacott of the University of Kansas, provides a forum for researchers and clinical practitioners interested in etiology, assessment, and treatment of anxiety and depression disorders of children and adolescents. Volume is moderate. The InterPsych discussion group was formerly called ANXIETY-DEPRESSION-YOUTH and hosted on a different server, but it has moved its location and changed its name.

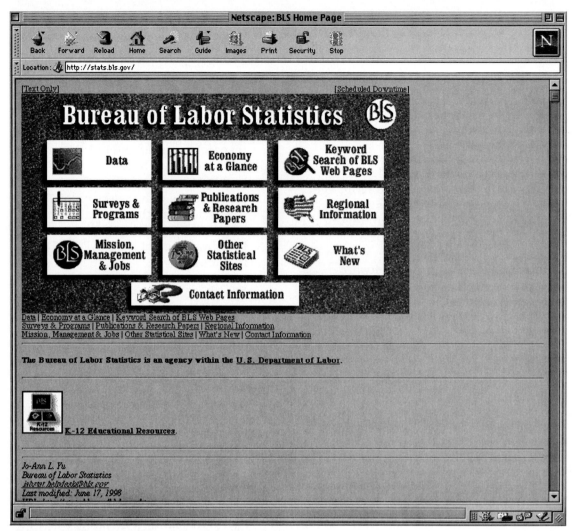

Source: The Bureau of Labor Statistics (http://stats.bls.gov).

Industrial and Organizational Psychology

Bad Human Factors Designs
http://www.baddesigns.com/

Michael J. Darnell has created this "scrapbook of illustrated examples of things that are hard to use because they do not follow human factors principles." It will appeal to everyone, but especially those involved in human factors. He divides the site by Things, Displays, Controls, and Signs & Names. For example, in the Controls section, "Hidden Controls" describes an elevator at a posh Los Angeles hotel whose buttons do not light up when pressed, and which gives no instructions for how to get to your floor. Darnell provides photos of the panel, explains what's wrong with the design, and then offers a way to correct the flaw. Other entries have intriguing names such as "Where Did We Park the Car?" and "Oh, That's How You Open It!"

Bureau of Labor Statistics
http://stats.bls.gov/

The Web site of the Bureau of Labor Statistics is an excellent source of statistics on the labor force; it includes the extensive LABSTAT database.

DIVERSITY-FORUM
Send e-mail to
MAJORDOMO@IGC.APC.ORG
Put in the body of the message:
SUBSCRIBE DIVERSITY-FORUM

This Majordomo mailing list provides a forum for those interested in human resource management, human relations in education, and social work. Other goals include stimulating research, developing diversity initiatives, and providing information on conferences, professional publications, and reviews in the area. The list is hosted by the National Association for Diversity Management (nadm@nadm.org) and is managed (though not moderated) by Frank H. Zade.

DOT Lookup I and II
Elliott & Fitzpatrick, Inc.
PO Box 1945
Atlanta, GA 30603
(706) 548-8161

DOT Lookup (for DOS) enables quick access to worker trait information based on the Dictionary of Occupational Titles. The database can be searched by DOT Code, industrial designation, work field, and other characteristics. The company also offers other software products to facilitate job classification and counseling for workers, such as Labor Market Access Plus 1992 and a CD-ROM containing information from the U.S. Department of Labor.

EA
Send e-mail to EA-
REQUEST@WEBCOM.COM or EAP.COM?
Put in the body of the message:
SUBSCRIBE EA Yourname

The Employee Assistance Counselor's Internet Discussion List (EA for short) is for those with an interest in employee counseling and psychological

interventions in the workplace. A number of professional associations, managed care companies, and corporations participate, along with university faculty and individuals. Managed by Bob Fleming, the list is used for discussion, job postings, calls for papers, book reviews, and exchanges of ideas about training.

EAWOP-L
Send e-mail to
LISTSERV@HEARN.NIC.SURFNET.NL
Put in the body of the message:
SUBSCRIBE EAWOP-L Yourname

This is the mailing list for the European Association of Work and Organizational Psychology.

IOOB-L
Send e-mail to
LISTSERV@UGA.CC.UGA.EDU
Put in the body of the message:
SUBSCRIBE IOOB-L Yourname

The industrial psychology forum is relatively inactive, though its purpose is to provide a forum for industrial and organizational psychologists.

Job Analysis and Personality Assessment (Virginia Tech)
http://harvey.psyc.vt.edu/

This Web site, created by R. J. Harvey, offers downloadable software, data, and documents dealing with job analysis and classification and personality assessment, along with links to related Web sites.

OBTS-L
Send e-mail to LISTSERV@BUCKNELL.EDU
Put in the body of the message:
SUBSCRIBE OBTS-L Yourname

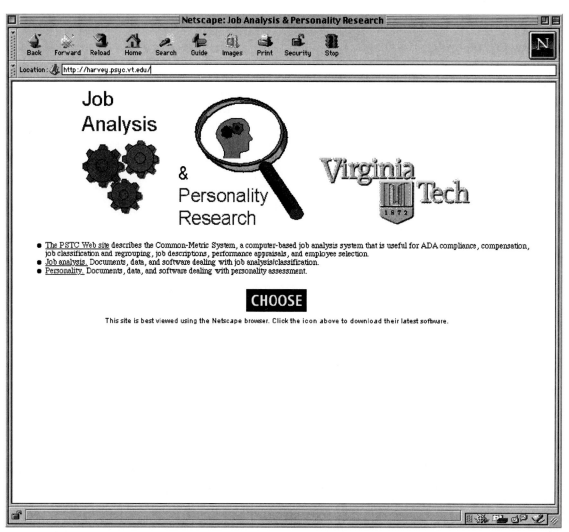

Location: http://harvey.psyc.vt.edu/

Job Analysis

& Personality Research

Virginia Tech

- The PSTC Web site describes the Common-Metric System, a computer-based job analysis system that is useful for ADA compliance, compensation, job classification and regrouping, job descriptions, performance appraisals, and employee selection.
- Job analysis. Documents, data, and software dealing with job analysis/classification.
- Personality. Documents, data, and software dealing with personality assessment.

CHOOSE

This site is best viewed using the Netscape browser. Click the icon above to download their latest software.

Job Analysis & Personality Research (http://harvey.psyc.vt.edu). Robert J. Harvey, Ph.D, Associate Professor, Virginia Polytechnic Institute and State University. Reprinted by permission.

This LISTSERV mailing list is sponsored by the Organizational Behavior Teaching Society and will be of interest to teachers of industrial and organizational psychology. Textbooks, teaching strategies, and resources in organizational psychology are discussed.

Society for Consumer Psychology
http://www.cob.ohio-state.edu/scp/

Behavioral scientists of all kinds belong to this professional organization,

which has close ties to the APA's Division 23 (Consumer Psychology). This Web site is very basic, but it provides the essential information about the SCP, including its most recent online newsletter in full text, conference announcements, and calls for papers.

The Society for Industrial and Organizational Psychology
http://www.siop.org/

This site is a good example of how an organization can create a simple but powerful presence on the Web. It includes links that are current and useful such as conference feedback postings, tapes from conferences, e-mail addresses for members, a sign-up form for committee volunteers, and, of course, full-text, archived issues of its newsletter, *TIP, The Industrial Psychologist.*

Psychology and the Law

The American Academy of Psychiatry and the Law
http://www.cc.emory.edu/AAPL/

The AAPL is the professional organization for forensic psychologists, but, even if you're not one of them, this site still has useful resources. There is a searchable database of the *Journal of the Academy of Psychiatry and the Law* (1973 to the present, with abstracts available from 1986), as well as sections on ethics, training in forensic psychiatry, criminal and civil issues, annual meetings, fellowships, and resources such as government links and Web sites of other organizations. They welcome questions, which are answered by member volunteers but do not represent official organization opinions.

American Psychology-Law Society
http://www.unl.edu/ap-ls/

The field of psychology and law is gaining in popularity, and this site, supported by the University of Nebraska's Law-Psychology Program, is the field's virtual headquarters. Here you will find general information about psychology and law, where to study, conference information – yes, there's a conference – and lots of links to papers and syllabi from programs around the country. The society publishes a journal, which can be downloaded using an Acrobat reader.

Federal Bureau of Investigation
http://www.fbi.gov/

This site contains information about crime and law enforcement, including in-depth analyses of high-profile cases.

FORENS-L
Send e-mail to MAILSERV@ACC.FAU.EDU
Put in the body of the message:
SUBSCRIBE FORENS-L Yourname

The Forensic Medicine and Sciences mailing list is an unmoderated and very active discussion targeted to forensic aspects of the social and behavioral sciences, including exchanges about the role of the expert witness and the presentation of evidence in court. The conversations are professional, and postings have explored a wide range of forensic topics, from conferences and workshops to software.

Legal Issues in the Online World

As the online world grows exponentially, governments ponder what kind of medium this actually is and how (or if) it should be regulated. In the United States, for example, the Communications Decency Act of 1996 triggered a storm of protest, especially among Internet users concerned about free speech and First Amendment rights. The act was eventually struck down through a unanimous Supreme Court decision, but the debate about whether and how much government should regulate online activity continues. For those who want to keep up with legal issues involving Internet and online services, here are some resources:

American Civil Liberties Union Home Page
http://www.aclu.org

The Benton Foundation
http://www.benton.org

The Electronic Frontier Foundation
http://www.eff.org

Ralph Nader and the Consumer Project on Technology
http://www.essential.org/cpt/telecom/telecom.html

International Society of Political Psychology
http://ispp.org/

The ISPP is concerned with the scholarly study of the relationship between politics and psychology. Its site offers a wide range of information on the topic, including full-text archives of its newsletter and annual meeting reports. There are links to course syllabi, the membership directory, and further resources in political psychology.

U.S. Supreme Court Decisions
http://www.law.cornell.edu/supct/

Cornell University's Legal Information Institute has graciously made available all the Supreme Court decisions and opinions since 1990 and more than 850 of the most influential historic decisions. The historic decisions are also available on CD-ROM. In addition, this site offers access to a variety of related publications.

Statistics and Experimental Research Tools

Automated Assessment Associates
http://www.softsolutions.com/autoasas/

Here are two automation products that streamline the assessment process. The first is called Scores-It-All 6.0P for Windows. It automates the scoring of any multiple-choice or true-false test and handles up to 1,000 items with 200 scales. No programming skills are needed to run the program.

The second is called the MMPI/MMPI-2 Adult Interpretive Report for Windows and is sold only to licensed psychologists. It interprets both the

MMPI-2 and MMPI and automatically converts MMPI-2s into their approximate MMPI equivalents. It generates a report that can be saved as a DOS file for editing with a word-processing program.

Bill Trochim's Center for Social Research Methods
http://trochim.human.cornell.edu/

Trochim, a professor of human services, developed this site not only for his students and colleagues at Cornell, but also for anyone involved in applied social research and evaluation. One of the tools available is Selecting Statistics, which Trochim calls an "online advisor." The program asks questions about your research and suggests statistical approaches and software based on your answers.

Trochim's site also features lecture slides, sample student projects, discussion groups, and links to research resources.

COSMIC
The University of Georgia
382 East Broad Street
Athens, GA 30602-4272
(706) 542-3265
http://www.cosmic.uga.edu

COSMIC is a registered trademark of NASA, and it distributes certain software products that may interest psychology students and professionals. One is CLIPS (C Language Integrated Production System), a development environment for the creation of expert systems, designed to allow research on artificial intelligence. Another is NETS, which is software for the development and evaluation of neural networks. Other software available through COSMIC includes MAT (Multi-attribute Task Battery for Human Operator Workload and Strategic Behavior Research) and PWC (Pairwise Comparison Software).

DADisp 4.1
DSP Development Corporation
One Kendall Square
Cambridge, MA 02139
(800) 424-3131
http://www.dadisp.com/

DADisp 4.1 is software that assists users with data collection and analysis, appropriate for scientists and engineers. A demo copy can be downloaded from the Web site.

Datasim
Drake R. Bradley
Desktop Press
90 Bardwell St.
Lewiston, ME 04240
(207) 786-4113
dbradley@abacus.bates.edu

Datasim is a general purpose data simulator for generating randomized datasets for various research designs. It can be used for computer-aided instruction, classroom demonstrations of sampling theory, and Monte Carlo research. The program has several statistical procedures such as ANOVA. Illustrations of the way Datasim is used have appeared in a number of issues of *Behavior Research, Methods, Instrumentation, and Computers*. Versions are available for IBM-compatible PCs ($45) or the Macintosh ($65). Site licenses are available.

Electronic Questionnaire Manager
A. and S. Sharpe
4 Drovers Way
Peebles EH45 9BN
Scotland
http://www.sharpeware.com

This DOS shareware program, available in many shareware repositories, provides a tool to create and analyze simple questionnaires. A network version is available. The user can enter questions into the program, creating a file that is used for input. Subjects can then be asked to take the computer-based survey, and their results will be appended to a different ASCII file. A sample questionnaire is provided with the program showing the different kinds of questions that can be included. One type is called "bar," and it provides a Likert-type scale in which the subject places a pointer on a bar with corresponding values between 1 and 10. Another type is the "follow-on," which permits some control over question presentation and branching. For example, the subject will see the follow-on question only if he or she responds in a certain way to a previous question. Registration for a single user is $15 plus shipping and includes a manual. A $25 network license is also available, which would facilitate using the program to collect responses from subjects simultaneously.

Experimental Run Time System (ERTS)
BeriSoft Corporation
Jörg Beringer
Wildenbruchstr. 49
60431 Frankfurt am Main, Germany
+49 (0)69 524248
http://www.compuserve.com/homepages/b erisoft/
ERTS@BeriSoft.F.Eunet.de
ERTS is powerful and feature-rich software designed to change an IBM-compatible PC into a test station particularly suited to research on cognition, perception, and other areas in which precise control of stimulus presentation and response recording is needed. The program uses a special definition language to identify the data objects, parameters for individual trials, blocks of trials, and the experimental session. Examples of research paradigms that can be implemented through ERTS include Sternberg memory research, mental rotation, visual search, vigilance,

Stroop color interference, Posner matching task, mathematical processing tasks, pursuit tracking tasks, and others. Experimenters can use visual (with 256 colors in the new version, called ERTSVIPL) or auditory stimuli (with a sound card), and they can collect responses from their subjects via the keyboard, mouse, joystick, or some other external device. Data from experiments are stored in ASCII readable files for analysis. The flexibility and richness of ERTS make it appropriate for an undergraduate psychology lab or for researchers. A downloadable demo is available on the Web site, and licenses start at about $950 for two machines.

GENSTAT
Socware, Inc.
1789 Colby Street
Brockport, NY 14420
(716) 352-1986
fhalley@acspr1.acs.brockport.edu
GENSTAT is a student data generation program for DOS that produces data sets for students to use in a research methods or social statistics course, using variable names and population parameters supplied by the instructor. Simulated data sets are generated separately for each student so each person has his or her own information to work with, and answer sheets are provided for the instructor for grading purposes. Resulting data files can also be exported to other statistical packages for further analysis.

Hudson Data Collection Program
Walter W. Hudson
WALMYR Publishing Co.
PO Box 6229
Tallahassee, FL 32314-6229
Voice: (850) 383-0045
http://www.syspac.com/~walmyr/
HDCP is Windows software designed to facilitate data entry for

researchers. The software enables the researcher to set up the assessment instruments, enter the data from respondents, and then analyze them using a statistics program. The author is also offering a new Windows software program called Computer Assisted Social Services (CASS).

MACPSYCH

Send e-mail to
MACPSYCH-REQUEST@STOLAF.EDU
Put in the body of the message:
Your name and a request to join.
(The request process is not handled by automated software so no special syntax is needed.)

Chuck Huff of the Department of Psychology at St. Olaf College moderates this mailing list and other resources for people interested in using the Macintosh computer in psychology teaching and research. An archive of Macintosh software written by members of the group is also maintained and can be accessed via anonymous ftp to ftp.stolaf.edu in the pub/macpsych directory.

E-Prime

Psychology Software Tools
2014 Monongahela Avenue
Pittsburgh, PA 15216
(412) 271-5040
http://www.pstnet.com/
info@pstnet.com

E-Prime is a cross-platform experiment generator studio, the planned successor to products described in the last edition of *Psych Online* called MEL Professional and PsyScope. The program (and its predecessors) help you develop computer-based psychology experiments. The new version features wizards that can walk you through development of a wide range of experiments that can be run on Macintosh or Intel computers. For information about the earlier freeware version of PsyScope, developed by Brian

MacWhinney and his colleagues, see the entry under PsyScope.

Methodologist's Toolchest Professional

Sage Publications Software
2455 Teller Road
Thousand Oaks, CA 91320
(805) 499-1325
http://www.sagepub.com/sagepage/mtc.htm

Idea Works offers a suite of Windows software products designed to provide decision support tools for researchers. Statistical Navigator Professional, for example, helps select the appropriate statistic for a project and uses some artificial intelligence in the process. Ex-Sample helps the researcher identify sample size requirements, and WhichGraph offers advice on how to construct graphs to minimize bias. Hyper-Stat is a memory resident statistical dictionary.

Models 'n' Data

Doug Stirling
Department of Statistics
Massey University
Palmserton North, New Zealand
d.stirling@massey.ac.nz
http://smis-www.massey.ac.nz/personal/DStirlin/

Models 'n' Data is a program for Macintosh computers containing statistical exercises to help teach statistics, not just analyze data. It displays and analyzes real data and enables students to create and manipulate statistical models pertaining to topics such as confidence intervals and least squares extrapolation. The Web site provides information about the program and examples of the models.

The Monty Hall Three Door Dilemma
http://www.dcity.org/braingames/3doors/

Though it appears to be an amusing and diverting game, it offers a useful statistical tutorial using the simulation of the 3-door problem made famous in "Let's Make a Deal." The game allows you to choose one of three doors, and then Monty opens one of the two doors you did not choose. If there is nothing behind this one, you are now able to stick with your initial door or switch to the other closed door. The statistics underlying the best decision under these circumstances are complex and counterintuitive. This kind of game is covered in many statistics courses.

The Observer Video-Pro
Noldus Information Technology
Costerweg 5
PO Box 268
6700 AG Wageningen
The Netherlands
+ 31-(0) 8370-97677
info@noldus.ni
http://www.noldus.com

Noldus offers a number of feature-rich products for behavioral scientists who do observational research and want to perform sophisticated data collection and analysis of visual and auditory events. The Observer Video-Pro software, for example, turns a computer into a professional workstation for organizing, analyzing, and presenting video material. The system is used for a wide range of applications such as usability testing, labor and time studies, neuroscience, psychology, animal behavior, entomology, toxicology, and sports.

PinPoint   Logotron Software
http://www.logo.com/pinpoint/index.htm

This program creates electronic surveys and questionnaires with user-friendly dialog boxes and drag-and-drop interfaces. After you draw the area on the screen where you want your question to appear, you then double-click for the Question Details dialog box and enter the question, name, type of question, and possible answers (if it is multiple choice). You can then print the questionnaire or save it to disk. PinPoint can perform a variety of powerful numerical and statistical analyses of resulting data and then produce graphs from the data.

PsyScope
Brian MacWhinney, Jonathan Cohen, Matthew Flatt, and Jefferson Provost
Department of Psychology
Carnegie Mellon University
http://poppy.psy.cmu.edu/psyscope/

PsyScope is a free Macintosh program that provides an interactive graphic system for experimental design and control, relying on scripts. Use of the program is described in Cohen, J.D., MacWhinney, B., Flatt, M., & Provost, J. (1993). PsyScope: A new graphic interactive environment for designing psychology experiments. *Behavioral Research Methods, Instruments and Computers, 25*(2), 257-271. All the files needed can be downloaded from the Web site, including the manuals for programmers and developers. A hardware add-on to PsyScope, called the CMU Button Box, is also available that has a separate microprocessor, push buttons, LED displays, outputs to the Macintosh and other devices, additional input lines, and a voice-activated relay, for about $500. PsyScope's successor is E-Prime, expected to be released in 1998. See the entry under E-Prime for more details.

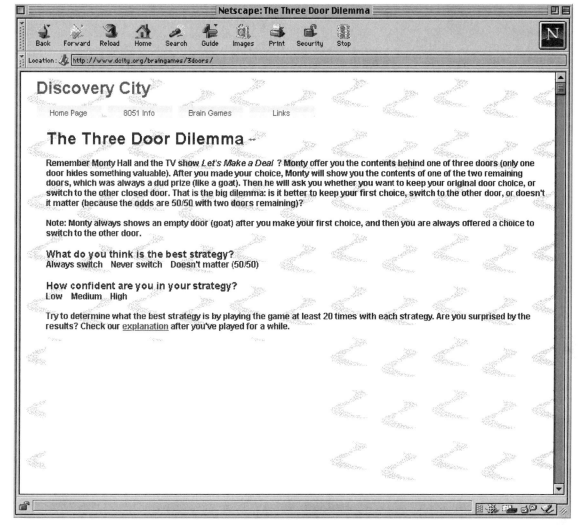

Monty Hall Three Door Dilemma (http://www.dcity.org/braingames/3doors). Reprinted by permission.

ResearchRandomizer
http://www.wesleyan.edu/spn/random/
rr.htm

   Geoffrey C. Urbaniak at Wesleyan University created ResearchRandomizer as an easy way to do random sampling or to assign subjects to experimental conditions. The Web site provides a color-coded tutorial to explain the many ways this program can be used. The tutorial takes about 10 minutes to complete, and then you can go right to the form on the site to begin using ResearchRandomizer. This program uses a JavaScript random number generator.

SCRT
Patrick Onghena and G. van Damme, University of Leuven, Belgium
Distributed by iec *Pro*GAMMA
http://indy1.gamma.rug.nl/index.html

   Single-Case Randomization Tests (SCRT) allows the user to design single-case experiments and perform graphical and statistical analyses on the data collected. It supports alternating treatment designs, AB designs, multiple baseline designs, and customized approaches. The program contains a number of features to support the single-case approach, such as nonparametric procedures in which a bottom-up methodology is used to analyze the data on the individual level first and then integrate the results at the group level later. In addition to statistical tests, the program supports graphical analyses and a variety of plots.

The Society for Computers in Psychology
http://www.lafayette.edu/allanr/scip.html
The purpose of this association, formed in 1971, is to increase and diffuse knowledge of the use of computers in psychological research. Membership costs $20 ($10 for students). The Web site provides information on its conferences, announcements of coming events, and calls for papers.

Sources of Statistical Software

The range of statistical software available for psychology students, faculty, and practitioners is mind-boggling. A search of the shareware collection on CompuServe alone using "statistics" as the search word came up with more than 300 hits. The following list features some of the most popular shareware and commercial software in use by students and professionals in psychology. Many offer demo diskettes, brochures, and extensive literature.

CSS: Statistica Software
Statsoft (on CD-ROM for Windows)
2300 East 14th Street
Tulsa, OK 74104
(918) 749-1119
info@statsoftinc.com
http://www.statsoftinc.com

Minitab Inc.
3081 Enterprise Drive
State College, PA 16801
(814) 238-3280

http://www.minitab.com

Multivariate Software, Inc.
4924 Balboa Blvd. #368
Encino, CA 91316
(800) 301-4456
http://www.mvsoft.com

NCSS 97 for Windows
NCSS
329 N 1000 E.
Kaysville, UT 84037
(800) 898-6109
http://www.ncss.com

SAS Institute Inc.
SAS Campus Drive
Cary, NC 27513
(919) 677-8000
http://www.sas.com

SPSS
SPSS, Inc.
444 North Michigan Avenue
Chicago, IL 60611-3962
(800) 543-2185
http://www.spss.com

Stat-100 (Windows)
Biosoft
PO Box 10938
Ferguson, MO 63135
(314) 524-8029
or
37 Cambridge Place
Cambridge, CB2 1NS, UK
+44 (0) 1223-368622

StatLib
http://lib.stat.cmu.edu/
The Statistics Department at Carnegie Mellon University hosts this important hub for distributing statistical software, datasets, and related information via Web downloading, e-mail, and FTP.

StatMost for Windows
Data Axiom Software Inc.
3701 Wilshire Blvd.
Suite 1122
Los Angeles, CA 90010
(213) 383-9973

StatView 4.5
SAS Institute Inc.
Attn: StatView Sales & Marketing
2 Embarcadero Center, Suite 200
San Francisco, CA 94111-3834
(415) 623-2032
info@statview.com
http://www.abacus.com/

SYSTAT
(now owned by SPSS – see above)

True Epistat
Epistat Services
1090 Lang Road, #4203
Portland, TX 78374
(512) 777-0209
epistatinc@aol.com

Sources of Funding for Psychology Research

The resources listed in this section are not just for high-powered researchers with laboratories and a long list of scholarly publications. Students who want to obtain funding for internships or small projects should also examine these sites. Several of the megasites listed in chapter 3 also contain some information for students seeking research funding.

Community of Science
http://www.cos.com
Community of Science in Baltimore, Maryland, offers a range of services to scientists. Examples include a database of grant awards from NIH, NSF, and a few other agencies; a database of researchers searchable by subject area of interest; and an online version of *Commerce Business Daily*. The emphasis is mainly on the natural sciences, rather than behavioral or social, but people involved in biology and behavior should find the service useful.

FEDIX
http://web.fie.com/fedix/index.html
FEDIX stands for Federal Information Exchange, Inc., and the organization is sponsored by a long list of federal agencies. It serves as an "information bridge" by providing comprehensive online information on federal agency opportunities to research and higher education communities. By accessing this Web site, you will be able to register as a FEDIX user (free of charge) and receive e-mail on grant opportunities relevant to your research areas. The Federal Opportunities Alert program is a service of FEDIX that allows you to create a personal interest profile using a keyword thesaurus. Once you are registered with a keyword list, FEDIX will e-mail you the results of a daily search of the federal opportunities that match. In psychology, I'd suggest you start with the broadest category (all psychology) and then narrow your keyword profile if you receive too many bulletins, though so far there doesn't seem to be any danger of overload. You will need to enter your e-mail address and a password to register and maintain your profile.

GrantsNet
http://www.grantsnet.org/
GrantsNet provides a searchable database of more than 350 sources for funding for training in the biological and medical sciences. You can search by a vast array of specialties. Registration is free but required for the search, which can be modified by number of applicants, field of study, and educational level. This site is co-sponsored by the American Association for the Advancement of Science and the Howard Hughes Medical Institute.

National Science Foundation
http://www.nsf.gov/

NSF's site includes a database of awards and publications, a full text of selected publications, film and video catalog, and information about NSF programs and grants.

SRA's GrantsWeb
http://web.fie.com/cws/sra/sra.htm

The Society of Research Administrators Web site includes a subsection called GrantsWeb that has considerable depth. There are hundreds of links divided into four main areas: Government Resources, with links to practically every federal agency; General Resources, with links to journals and grant forms; Policy Information and Circulars, which features a writing guide and legal information; and Private Funding Resources, with its comprehensive list of private foundation links.

Other Resources

Smaller subdisciplines of psychology that have fewer online materials, a few psychology-related games, some government sites, and resources that defy categorization are listed in this group.

Center for the Study of Computer Communication
http://cscc.clarion.edu/

Clarion University of Pennsylvania sponsors this Web site designed to facilitate research on the impact of computer technology on communication behavior. Under the direction of Scott A. Kuehn, the site offers information on research on computer communication, links to other resources, and information

on how to set up your own Web site so you can experience the impact of computer communication yourself.

Conversational Hypertext Access Technology (CHAT)
http://debra.dgbt.doc.ca/chat

Thomas Whalen and Andrew Patrick at Industry Canada developed this information retrieval technology. The site offers a Web-based dialog capability through which you can enter questions in natural language and receive computerized responses. In the "Epilepsy" dialog, for example, you can enter "What causes epilepsy?" and receive a very rational reply. There are several interfaces and a number of topics from which you can choose, including a mystery conversation, a dialog about sex, and a tutorial in which you use natural language to discuss the elements of job interviews with a tutor. It's fun to examine the responses of the computer and compare them with those that might be provided by a human. Sometimes you just can't tell the difference. A demo version of the software is available to download from the Web site.

ECOPSYCHOLOGY
**Send e-mail to
LISTSERV@MAELSTROM.STJOHNS.EDU
Put in the body of the message:
SUBSCRIBE ECOPSYCHOLOGY Yourname**

Moderated by Claudia Robinson, the ecopsychology mailing list is intended to provide a forum for discussing the interface between psychology and ecology. The list includes an eclectic group of participants who share an interest in the role of human behavior in the fate of the Earth but who differ widely in approaches and perspectives. Claudia encourages all participants to introduce themselves before posting any messages.

Portrait of a New Mailing List Moderator

Claudia Robinson, born and raised in Germany and a graduate student at Clemson, decided to start a mailing list on the topic of ecopsychology so that people interested in this esoteric field would have an efficient means of communication. She wants to add more resources, such as a Web site, as time and money permit, and she hopes the list will serve as a springboard for these other initiatives. She volunteered with the Peace Corps in Botswana and would like to create an online ecopsychology/deep ecology university.

Claudia doesn't have many technical problems with her list server, as so many list owners do, but she does have problems with the participation and philosophical orientations of her subscribers. The majority post spiritual messages, but this scares away the more academic and analytical types who want to discuss research and don't want to wade through endless confessional posts. She is not sure how to "encourage a dialogue between those representing the intellect and those representing the heart," as she puts it. Bridging the gap between the intellectual and intuitive domains is a major hurdle for a list like this, and for many others like it in psychology. A discussion forum is a free-form coffeehouse, and participants have more control than the moderator does over the direction and focus of the group. Most moderators stand back and filter only the obviously irritating or inappropriate posts. Unlike most list owners, Claudia actively tries to find out why people sign off ECOPSYCHOLOGY to learn more about their interests and how she might shape the group to fit a broader range of needs. For example, she suggested that the group invite some guest speakers. Like most other list owners, Claudia does all this work without reward other than the satisfaction of bringing people together who have something they want to discuss.

ENVBEH-L
Send e-mail to LISTPROC@DUKE.POLY.EDU
Put in the body of the message:
SUBSCRIBE ENVBEH-L Yourname

The Environment and Human Behavior discussion group, managed by Richard Wener, encourages discussions of the relationship between people and the physical environment, including architectural and interior environments. Topics also include pollution, disasters, and human responses to environmental conditions.

ETHOLOGY
Send e-mail to
LISTSERV@SEGATE.SUNET.SE
Put in the body of the message:
SUBSCRIBE ETHOLOGY Yourname

Jarmo Saarikko of University of Helsinki in Finland manages this list for professionals and students interested in animal behavior and behavioral ecology. The group is also linked to the USENET newsgroup sci.bio.ethology.

FacePrints
http://www-psych.nmsu.edu/
~vic/faceprints/

Victor Johnson in the Psychology Department at New Mexico State University created this page to collect data on people's judgments of facial beauty. Visitors rank 16 male and 16 female faces on attractiveness on a scale from 1 to 9. The program follows a genetic analogy and the algorithms assign "relative fitness values" based on visitors' ratings. From the first generation of random faces, the program evolves a composite face for each new generation, using the general principles of natural selection that would assume that more attractive people would leave more offspring. The "fairest of us all" changes with each generation of experimental results, and you can view these fine looking (but imaginary) faces of men and women at the site.

FEDWORLD
http://www.fedworld.gov/
FEDWORLD is a good site to begin exploring the catacombs of government resources on the Internet. It has links to most of the other sites and information about federal jobs.

Go Ask Alice
http://www.columbia.edu/cu/healthwise/alice.html
The Healthwise office of the Health Education Division of Columbia University Health Services maintains an online question and answer service for health-related queries. You can search its Q and A archives using keywords to see if Alice already answered your question, or you can post your own question anonymously. Replies are public, though your name is omitted, and available through the archive. It warns that you might have to wait a month for an answer, and some questions are not answered at all. When Alice does answer a question, the answer is sound and comprehensive. Many questions are related to psychology and emotional well-being. Examples include queries about seasonal affective disorder, grief, depression, and shyness. Alice is

particularly careful about suggesting professional help when it may be warranted.

Government Information Locator Service
http://info.er.usgs.gov/public/gils/
This site offers an index to government information in print and electronic forms.

Human-Computer Interaction Laboratory
http://www.cs.umd.edu/projects/hcil/
A project team at the University of Maryland at College Park is studying the interaction between humans and computers, and its Web site provides a description of the project, as well as a number of papers and technical reports on the subject.

Mind Games
http://weber.u.washington.edu/~jlks/mindgame.html
Jordan Schwartz offers a selection of games and puzzles that have a psychological twist. Examples include "Mind Control," "The Math Game," and "The Pick-a-Number Game."

Narrative Psychology
http://web.lemoyne.edu/~hevern/narpsych.html
Vincent Hevern in the Psychology Department at Le Moyne College in New York has created an intriguing site with an extensive bibliography, links to Internet resources, lists of conferences, and other information on the subject of narrative psychology, which focuses on the "storied nature of human conduct."

The bibliography is particularly impressive. The site also includes a large, annotated collection of links to other resources in psychology (http://web.lemoyne.edu/ ~hevern/psychref.html). Hevern warns that he is on sabbatical during 1998-1999 and may not do much updating, but the site's URL will remain the same.

NUVUPSY
Send e-mail to
LISTSERV@MAELSTROM.STJOHNS.EDU
Put in the body of the message:
SUBSCRIBE NUVUPSY Yourname

NUVUPSY (new view psychology) focuses on sociological, political, and existential issues in psychology, and a major discussion topic is the "therapeutic state." Participants express viewpoints that are critical of institutional psychiatry, and the list promotes alternative explanations of unwanted, deviant behavior. The list is affiliated with the Thomas S. Szasz Cybercenter for Liberty and Responsibility (http://rdz.acor.org/szasz/) and has a board of advisors that includes professionals from a range of disciplines.

POWR-L
Send e-mail to
LISTSERV@URIACC.URI.EDU
Put in the body of the message:
SUBSCRIBE POWR-L Yourname

Cosponsored by Division 35 of the American Psychological Association, the Psychology of Women Resources List facilitates discussion of women's issues, teaching strategies, upcoming conferences and events, calls for papers, and relevant reference material. Postings are not filtered, but the moderator, Kat Quina of the Department of Psychology at the University of Rhode Island, will unsubscribe participants who submit messages inconsistent with the goals of the discussion.

PSYART
Send e-mail to
LISTSERV@NERVM.NERDC.UFL.EDU
Put in the body of the message:
SUBSCRIBE PSYART Yourname

http://www.clas.ufl.edu/ipsa/intro.htm

This eclectic discussion group explores the relationship between psychology and art. It is remarkably active, and participants engage in debates about the psychological meaning of artistic works, the psychology of art lovers, and an assortment of other loosely related topics. I subscribed to this list and stayed on for far longer than I intended because the level of discussion was quite high and participants brought some fascinating interdisciplinary perspectives to the topic.

The list's moderator, Norm Holland of the English Department at the University of Florida, also maintains a related Web site rich with materials on the relationship between psychology and the arts.

Psychology of Religion Page
http://www.psych-web.com/psyrelig
Michael E. Nielsen of Georgia Southern University created this site on the psychology of religion. It includes an introduction to the topic as it is studied by researchers, summaries of research by psychologists on how religion influences people's lives, descriptions of research methods, and some tips for students who are interested in pursuing this area in graduate school. The site is housed within PsychWeb described in chapter 4. This is an academic site that scrupulously avoids advocacy of one religion over another, emphasizing the study of religion from the psychological point of view.

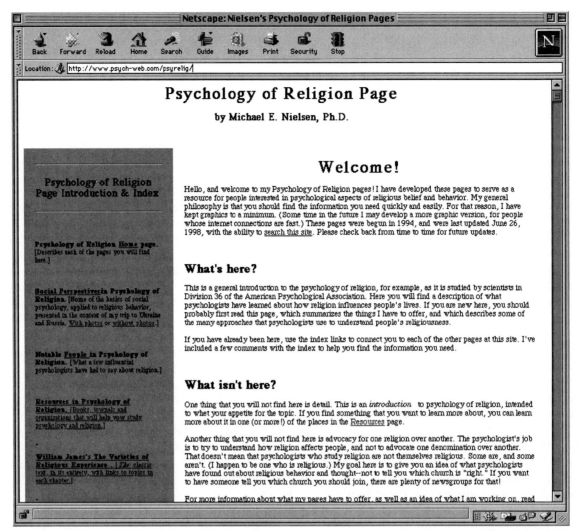

Psychology of Religion Page (http://www.psych-web.com/psyrelig/) Reprinted by permission of Michael E. Nielsen.

The Psychology Page
http://www.cs.washington.edu/homes/raj/psych.html

This site offers some psychology games for students with time on their hands and is currently looking for a new owner. Games have been archived, however. One such game is called "King for a Day," and visitors have entered their responses to some convoluted questions about the kinds of experiences they would accept or refuse if they were king for 24 hours. Another game, called "The Literature Page," invited visitors to contribute some text to an ongoing story. All contributions to the games were posted anonymously.

Radical Psychology Network
http://www.uis.edu/~radpsy/

RADICAL-PSYCHOLOGY-NETWORK
Send e-mail to
MAILBASE@MAILBASE.AC.UK
Put in the body of the message:
SUBSCRIBE RADICAL-PSYCHOLOGY-NETWORK Yourname

The Internet is a place where alternative viewpoints can be aired to the world, and RadPsyNet fills this kind of function. The organization was founded in 1993 at the Toronto APA Convention by a handful of people whose goal is to create a better society without social injustice and to challenge the status quo of psychology. The site includes a newsletter, membership statistics, various documents relating to radical psychology, course syllabi, and a variety of other links.

RESEARCH
Send e-mail to johngr@cmhcsys.com and ask to be put on the list.

This mailing list focuses on the psychology of the Internet, exploring research, theory, and practice. The group was started in 1996, and its membership skyrocketed almost immediately, indicating the widespread interest in the subject. Topics include the psychology of flame wars, online support groups, psychological surveys on the Internet, Internet Addiction Disorder, and other subjects that relate psychology to the online world. One discussion examined the hypothesis that men and women tend to use different language on the Net.

Smithsonian Institution
http://www.si.edu/

The Web site provides access to the research catalogs of the Smithsonian Institution, which contain information about books, serials, archives, manuscripts, and other kinds of documents in the collection.

Synchronicity and Chance
alt.psychology.synchronicity

The unmoderated newsgroup is an offbeat collection of postings, mostly about unusual coincidences and other events that appear to have some significance not superficially apparent.

Some postings relate personal experiences, such as the one that told of the extraordinarily frequent appearance of the number 167 in the person's life. Others offer psychological interpretation for coincidences.

WEBPSYCH
Send e-mail to johngr@cmhcsys.com and ask to be put on the list.

The mailing list is a resource for people creating and managing psychology-related Web sites. Topics include how to distribute information about your site, how to avoid duplicating online resources, and how to continue to offer free services.

The White House
http://www.whitehouse.gov/

The White House has been included in many lists of "cool sites," and it is still a showplace. It includes audio speeches along with their text versions, direct access to federal services, an Interactive Citizen's Handbook, and various tours of the White House. Some potentially useful material for psychology students includes the following:

http://www.pub.whitehouse.gov/WH/
Publications/html/Publications.html

From here you can find presidential speeches, recent policy briefings, briefings on jobs, and the text of the Health Security Act, National Information Infrastructure Initiative, National Performance Review, and a variety of others. You can also subscribe to daily publications by following the directions to send e-mail.

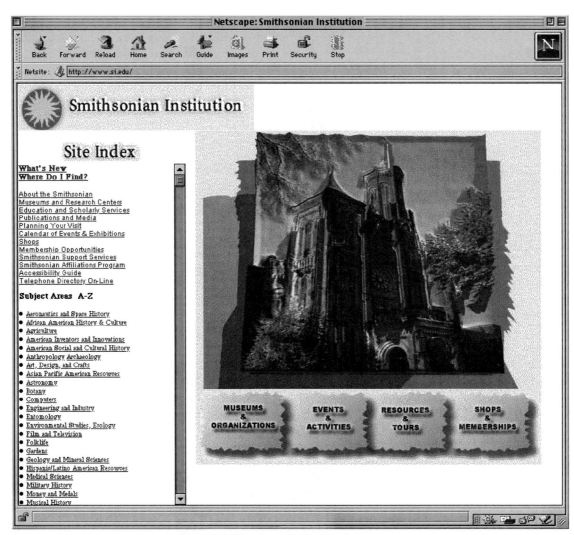

Source: The Smithsonian Institution Web Site (http://www.si.edu/).

http://www.whitehouse.gov/WH_Fellows/

This site describes the White House fellowship program and selection procedure, which may attract students interested in studying the relationship between psychology and politics.

Women's Studies: UMBC and Beyond

http://www-unix.umbc.edu/ ~korenman/wmst/

The Women's Studies Program at University of Maryland, Baltimore County, maintains an extensive list of links to online resources in the area of women's studies as part of its academic program. This site has a frequently updated list of electronic forums on women's issues, as well as numerous links to related Web sites and gophers.

The World's Fastest Moving Jokes, Legends, and Anecdotes

Social psychologists have an endless supply of material to study in the dynamics of social interaction within cyberspace. For example, the ease with which people can forward messages from electronic mailbox to mailbox and discussion list to list makes the online world a place where jokes, legends, and amusing anecdotes travel with lightning speed. There are so many newcomers joining the online community, or even veterans who recently subscribed to a particular discussion group and don't know its history, which these messages reappear with regularity. The newsgroups, forums, and mailing lists are all targets for people who begin with the line "I thought you all would find this amusing/horrifying/interesting/relevant...."

In some cases, the forwarded message is well received. In others, it incites a barrage of protests from other participants who saw the same forwarded message in many of the other groups to which they belong. Be careful about forwarding jokes or other materials to your fellow group members.

One message that flashed its way through most of the psychology-related lists took a satiric look at the growing number of automated, menu-based telephone services:

Hello, welcome to the Psychiatric Hotline.
If you are obsessive-compulsive, press 1, repeatedly.
If you are co-dependent, please ask someone to help you press 2.
If you have multiple personalities, press 2, 3, 4, and 5.
. . . and so on.

Another offered template prayers for people identified in each of the 16 Myers-Briggs types, such as

ESTJ: God, help me not to try to RUN everything. But if You need help, just ask.
INFP: God, help me to finish everything I sta
ISTJ: Lord help me to relax about insignificant details beginning tomorrow at 11:41:23 a.m. e.s.t.

A recurring story, apparently apocryphal, describes a woman who posted a highly valued cookie recipe from Neiman Marcus on the Internet because she was so outraged they charged her $250 for it without her consent. This cookie story reappears every few months and continues to delight newcomers, probably because it shows how the online world can create a highly informed, democratic environment where consumers can instantly communicate their dissatisfaction with any perceived corporate misdeeds.

The sheer volume of online material makes it difficult to sort, categorize, analyze, and test hypotheses about social dynamics. However, because the interactions are in electronic format, they will be an enormous advantage for social psychologists as they investigate human behavior and relationships in this worldwide forum.

6 Abnormal, Clinical, and Counseling Psychology

Computer-based and online resources for those interested in abnormal, clinical, and counseling psychology as well as other related mental health areas, are varied and extensive. They range from comprehensive FAQs, brochures, and encyclopedias to online therapy. This chapter covers quite a range of resources, such as discussion groups for researchers studying specific topics in clinical psychology to support groups for people with behavioral disorders. The first part of the chapter lists the academic and professional resources needed by students and professionals in these disciplines. The second section lists software resources for practitioners. The last section concentrates on resources designed to provide support and self-help.

Academic and Professional Resources

ADDICT-L
Send e-mail to
LISTSERV@KENTVM.KENT.EDU
Put in the body of the message:
SUBSCRIBE ADDICT-L Yourname
This very active open LISTSERV discussion group is directed toward researchers studying addiction processes and is not designed as a support group or forum for recovery. The discussion covers theories, treatments, and other scholarly topics. Although the group is targeted to researchers, quite a number of participants are addicts or in recovery and occasionally the discussion becomes highly charged. Archives are available.

Aesclepian Chronicles
Synergistic Health Center - Chapel Hill, North Carolina
http://www.forthrt.com/~chronicl/homepage.html

Aesclepian Chronicles is the electronic journal of the Synergistic Health Center, which specializes in the interaction of complementary and allopathic medicine. The approach takes a holistic strategy to medical problems, and the center relies on a health care team to treat the patient's body, mind, emotions, and spirit as a whole. The full text of the journal's articles is online, as are book reviews and links of similar interest.

AnyPsych Bookshop
19 East Putnam Avenue
Greenwich, CT 06830
Phone: (800) 211-5924
Fax: (203) 869-0633
http://www.behavior.net/AnyPsych/
E-mail: anypsych@behavior.net

This site promises to be able to find any book about mental health or applied behavioral science, even those that are now out of print. You can search by author or title or browse its sections, such as Neuropsychology, Cognitive & Behavioral Therapy, and the Bargain Bin. Ordering is by phone, fax, e-mail, or snail-mail. This service is co-sponsored by Just Books and Behavior OnLine.

APA Online – American Psychiatric Association

http://www.psych.org/

The American Psychiatric Association's Web site features psychiatric news such as legislative decisions and conference announcements and links to many practical resources such as a library, a list of APA members, and research resources. The site is also offering online courses, which psychiatrists can take to fulfill their CME requirement. Examples include "New Clinical Approaches for Treating Anxiety and Depression." In addition to the slide/audio program, there is a recommended reading list and a self-test.

Attention Deficit Disorder WWW Archive

http://www.realtime.net/cyanosis/add/

Meng Weng Wong started this comprehensive site of resources and publications on Attention Deficit Disorder (ADD). It is now maintained by Bill Scarborough and includes articles from ADDult News Online, tips on living with ADD, and the ADD FAQ.

audioPsych

http://www.audiopsych.com/

Mental Health Net and Behavior OnLine have teamed up to provide a way for psychologists to earn continuing education credits online with courses that use RealAudio, automatic slide presentations, and discussion forums. Courses are worth from one to twelve credit hours and cost about $10 to $15 per credit, but discounts are often offered. You can register and pay for courses online as well. As of this writing, credits are available only for psychologists and certified counselors,

not for social workers or psychiatrists (for psychiatrists, see the entry in this chapter under APA Online: American Psychiatric Association).

BEHAVIOR

**Send e-mail to
LISTSERV@ASUVM.INRE.ASU.EDU
Put in the body of the message:
SUBSCRIBE BEHAVIOR Yourname**

The Behavioral and Emotional Disorders in Children (BEHAVIOR) list is an open LISTSERV discussion group targeted at researchers, educators, students, and parents who have an interest in issues such as treatment and remediation, service providers, legal concerns, and general research in the area. The list has moderate activity. Archives are available.

Behavior OnLine

http://www.behavior.net/

The site's goal is to become the premiere Web gathering place for mental health professionals and applied behavioral scientists. Gilbert Levin, the site's founder, is a professor at the Albert Einstein College of Medicine who developed their program in health psychology. The creators intend to charge for some services at some point though many resources will continue to be offered for free. You can register to be a charter member online. The site offers Web-based discussion forum called "conversations" on therapy-related topics such as "Online Clinical Work" or "The Psychology of Cyberspace", and many are extremely active. "Shame and Affect Theory." Most have highly qualified and active moderators to facilitate the engaging online discussion. It also offers links to selected articles, and a call for papers from the new *Journal of Online Behavior*.

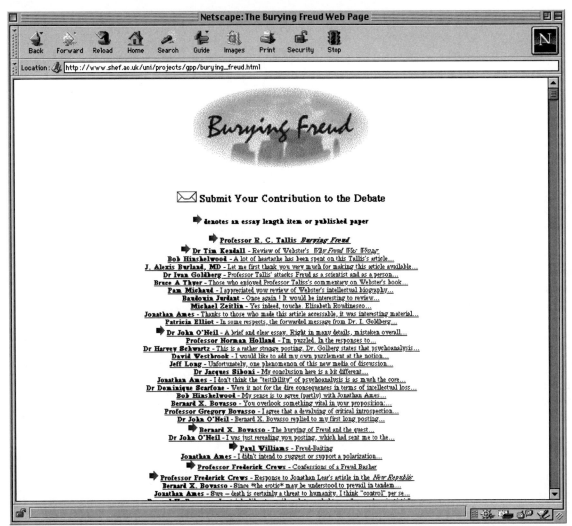

Location: http://www.shef.ac.uk/uni/projects/gpp/burying_freud.html

Burying Freud

✉ **Submit Your Contribution to the Debate**

➡ **denotes an essay length item or published paper**

➡ Professor R. C. Tallis *Burying Freud*
➡ **Dr Tim Kendall** - Review of Webster's *Why Freud Was Wrong*
Bob Hinshelwood - A lot of heartache has been spent on this Tallis's article...
J. Alexis Burland, MD - Let me first thank you very much for making this article available...
Dr Ivan Goldberg - Professor Tallis' attacks Freud as a scientist and as a person...
Bruce A Thyer - Those who enjoyed Professor Taliss's commentary on Webster's book...
Pam Michaud - I appreciated your review of Webster's intellectual biography...
Baudouin Jurdant - Once again ! It would be interesting to review...
Michael Zeitlin - Yes indeed, touche. Elisabeth Roudinesco...
Jonathan Ames - Thanks to those who made this article accessable, it was interesting material...
Patricia Elliot - In some respects, the forwarded message from Dr. I. Goldberg...
➡ **Dr John O'Neil** - A brief and clear essay. Right in many details, mistaken overall...
Professor Norman Holland - I'm puzzled. In the responses to...
Dr Harvey Schwartz - This is a rather strange posting. Dr. Golberg states that psychoanalysis...
David Westbrook - I would like to add my own puzzlement at the notion...
Jeff Long - Unfortunately, one phenomenon of this new media of discussion...
Dr Jacques Siboni - My conclusion here is a bit different...
Jonathan Ames - I don't think the "testibility" of psychoanalysis is as much the core...
Dr Dominique Scarfone - Were it not for the dire consequences in terms of intellectual loss...
Bob Hinshelwood - My sense is to agree (partly) with Jonathan Ames...
Bernard X. Bovasso - You overlook something vital in your proposition:...
Professor Gregory Bovasso - I agree that a devaluing of critical introspection...
Dr John O'Neil - Bernard X. Bovasso replied to my first long posting...
➡ **Bernard X. Bovasso** - The burying of Freud and the quest...
Dr John O'Neil - I was just rereading you posting, which had sent me to the...
➡ **Paul Williams** - Freud-Baiting
Jonathan Ames - I didn't intend to suggest or support a polarization...
➡ **Professor Frederick Crews** - Confessions of a Freud Basher
➡ **Professor Frederick Crews** - Response to Jonathan Lear's article in the *New Republic*
Bernard X. Bovasso - Since *the erotic* may be understood to prevail in tandem...
Jonathan Ames - Sure – death is certainly a threat to humanity. I think "control" per se...

Burying Freud (http://www.shet.ac.uk/uni/projects/gpp/burying_freud.html/). Reprinted by permission.

Brief Therapy
Subscribe from this Web site:
http://www.inetarena.com/~bneben

or

Send e-mail to majordomo@inetarena.com
Put in the body of the message:
SUBSCRIBE BRIEFTHERAPY

This is a fairly active list which focuses on the following types of therapy: Solution-Focused, Strategic, Structural, and MRI – DONE Brief Therapy. It is a place to discuss cases and raise issues relating to brief therapy and is useful for both professional therapists and students alike.

The companion Web site provides a detailed description of the list and an online subscription form.

Burying Freud
http://www.shef.ac.uk/uni/projects/gpp/
burying_freud.html

This intriguing site includes the full text of an article by R. C. Tallis that appeared in *The Lancet*. It explores the enormous 20th-century influence of Sigmund Freud and calls for a rational and fair assessment. Tallis boldly states, "Freud as a scientist, metapsychologist, and diagnostician of society emerges as a

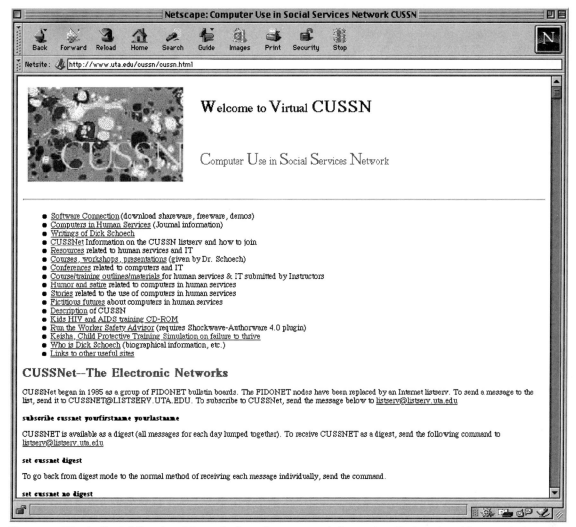

The browser window contains:

Netscape: Computer Use in Social Services Network CUSSN

Netsite: http://www.uta.edu/cussn/cussn.html

Welcome to Virtual CUSSN

Computer Use in Social Services Network

- Software Connection (download shareware, freeware, demos)
- Computers in Human Services (Journal information)
- Writings of Dick Schoech
- CUSSNet Information on the CUSSN listserv and how to join
- Resources related to human services and IT
- Courses, workshops, presentations (given by Dr. Schoech)
- Conferences related to computers and IT
- Course/training outlines/materials for human services & IT submitted by Instructors
- Humor and satire related to computers in human services
- Stories related to the use of computers in human services
- Fictitious futures about computers in human services
- Description of CUSSN
- Kids HIV and AIDS training CD-ROM
- Run the Worker Safety Advisor (requires Shockwave-Authorware 4.0 plugin)
- Keisha, Child Protective Training Simulation on failure to thrive
- Who is Dick Schoech (biographical information, etc.)
- Links to other useful sites

CUSSNet--The Electronic Networks

CUSSNet began in 1985 as a group of FIDONET bulletin boards. The FIDONET nodes have been replaced by an Internet listserv. To send a message to the list, send it to CUSSNET@LISTSERV.UTA.EDU. To subscribe to CUSSNet, send the message below to listserv@listserv.uta.edu

subscribe cussnet yourfirstname yourlastname

CUSSNET is available as a digest (all messages for each day lumped together). To receive CUSSNET as a digest, send the following command to listserv@listserv.uta.edu

set cussnet digest

To go back from digest mode to the normal method of receiving each message individually, send the command.

set cussnet no digest

Computer Use in Social Services Network (http://www.uta.edu/cussn.html/). Reprinted by permission from Dick Schoech, Professor, University of Texas at Arlington, School of Social Work.

quack." The site also includes reviews and analyses of the article and invites readers to mail their own responses to be posted on the Web site along with the original article. The site is an example of how the Internet makes radical changes in the way scholarly opinion is presented and debated.

Clinical Trials Listing Service
http://www.centerwatch.com/

Sponsored by CenterWatch, a multimedia publisher of clinical trial industry information, this Listing Service features sections for both professionals and patients alike. Professionals can check out profiles of research centers and industry providers, learn about job and educational opportunities, and keep current on clinical trial industry news. The patient site offers trial information listed by state and study and features an e-mail service that will alert you to new studies in your area of interest. Another valuable feature is a listing of currently approved FDA drugs.

ClinPSYC CD-ROM
http://www.apa.org/

Designed for researchers, practitioners, and students in clinical psychology, behavioral medicine, and other mental health professions,

ClinPSYC is a specialized CD-ROM database developed by the PsycINFO Department of the American Psychological Association. It features journal citations and abstracts, in a rolling 10-year file, selected from the PsycINFO master collection on the basis of their relevance to clinical psychology and medicine. APA recently reduced the subscription price for this product significantly, making it more accessible.

COGREHAB
Life Science Associates
One Fenimore Road
Bayport, NY 11705-2115
(516) 472-2111
lifesciassoc@pipeline.com
http://www.pipeline.com/~lifesciassoc

The company offers an extensive line of software and accessory products to assist with the process of cognitive rehabilitation, with modules on free recall, memory span, sequence recall, verbal memory, complex attention span, vigilance tasks, and others, as well as materials for cognitive assessment. Examples of hardware accessories include foot switches, finger extension switch, and a steering wheel to accompany its software to help patients relearn driving skills. Products are priced from $20 to $50.

Computers in Mental Health
http://www.ex.ac.uk/cimh/welcome.htm

Computers-in-Mental-Health
Send e-mail to Martin Briscoe (M.H.Briscoe@exeter.ac.uk) or Carl Littlejohns (csljohns@cix.compulink.co.uk) giving your name, e-mail address, occupation, and place of work.

The Web site, sponsored by the Royal College of Psychiatrists at the University of Exeter, is an outgrowth of the mailing list of the same name and includes a list of links to a variety of sites on the Internet that offer software related to the mental health professions. A very useful feature is the software database organized into categories such as analysis, billing, patient records, monitoring, assessment, and others. The entries include excellent information about each software package, and many carry reviews by users. The site also includes archives of the discussion group, links to some shareware products, and links to Web pages of the members of the mailing list.

The mailing list itself is open to professionals with an interest in computing and mental health.

COUNPSY
Send e-mail to
LISTSERV@UGA.CC.UGA.EDU
Put in the body of the message:
SUBSCRIBE COUNPSY Yourname

The Counseling Psychology LISTSERV mailing list, led by Rupert M. Perez of the University of Georgia, supports the exchange of ideas and issues related to the theory, practice, and science of counseling psychology. It is directed toward professionals in the field and advanced students. Topics include recent research, training issues, clinical issues in counseling, and discussions of collaborative projects.

CUSSN (Computer Use in Social Services Network)
http://www.uta.edu/cussn/cussn.html

This informal association of professionals offers a variety of resources to exchange information and experiences on the use of computers in the human services. The association publishes the journal *Computers in Human Services* and maintains this Web site with a collection of software descriptions pertinent to human service professionals in areas such as welfare and child protection, aging, developmental disabilities, data analysis, and therapy. Many of the software packages listed are demos, shareware, or freeware versions and are available for immediate downloading.

Cyber-Psych
http://www.cyber-psych.com

This site features an organized collection of online resources for psychological care and mental health. It includes therapist directories, mental health brochures, descriptions of mental health policies and assistance programs, and a variety of link pages. The creators have grouped resources according to categories such as domestic abuse, addictions, eating disorders, sexual abuse recovery, grief and loss, and sleep disorders, and visitors will be able to find many relevant links under each heading.

Department of Health and Human Services
http://www.os.dhhs.gov/

The Department of Health and Human Services maintains a very large site with information on health-related material and descriptions of various grant programs for research.

Discussion of Works and Theories of Carl Jung
alt.psychology.jung

This alternative, unmoderated forum offers some information about Jungian groups, poetry, and other resources, but much of the newsgroup involves conversations among participants offering humanistic advice to one another, such as "the journey is almost as important as the destination." The level of activity is relatively low for a psychology-related newsgroup – perhaps

because it is not the target of so many cross-postings.

Discussions on the Psychology of the Personality
alt.psychology.personality

This active newsgroup is an unmoderated, alternative forum for wide-ranging discussions of personality, with much interest in Myers-Briggs and other popular personality inventory systems, as well as less relevant discussions on topics such as reincarnation. If you don't know your ESTJs from your INFPs, you might miss the point of many postings. It includes the usual level of insults and flames and the inevitable barrage of cross-postings.

DIV12
Send e-mail to
LISTSERV@LISTSERV.NODAK.EDU
Put in the body of the message:
SUBSCRIBE DIV12 Yourname

This is the official discussion forum for the American Psychological Association's Division 12, open to all members and affiliates of the division. Moderated by Joseph Plaud of the University of North Dakota, who also moderates several other related discussion groups, the list provides an opportunity to share ideas related to the science and practice of clinical psychology.

Dr. Bob's Psychopharmacology Tips
http://uhs.bsd.uchicago.edu/dr-bob/tips/tips.html

Robert Hsiung, MD, Assistant Professor of Clinical Psychiatry at the University of Chicago, has amassed a large collection of tips about medications for both psychiatric and nonpsychiatric disorders. Tips have been culled from the Psycho-Pharm mailing list hosted by InterPsych and from Dr. Bob's personal collection.

Helping Others on the Net

John Grohol became interested in using the Internet to help people in trouble while still a graduate student in clinical psychology. After learning that his childhood best friend committed suicide, John became very depressed until he discovered the alt.support.depression newsgroup. The help and support he received from the group's participants pointed him toward his current full-time career. He now works for a mental health software developer and is in charge of the Web site Mental Health Net (http://www.cmhc.com/).

John never abandoned his interest in the online forums, though, and he will help others who want to start new newsgroups in the alt.support hierarchy if none of the existing groups quite fit. He facilitates several of the discussion forums, including the very active Psychology of the Internet mailing list, which discusses the psychological aspects of online behavior (see RESEARCH, chapter 5). Like others involved in this work, John never has enough time, but he certainly seems to get a great deal done.

The site is frames-based and fully searchable by term or by subject. Dr. Bob makes the disclaimer that these tips are from the experience of practicing psychiatrists and not necessarily scientifically tested.

EMBASE CD: Psychiatry
Elsevier Science
650 Avenue of the Americas
New York, NY 10011
(800) 457-3633
http://www.elsevier.com

The EMBASE CD-ROM includes more than 300,000 citations and abstracts from the much larger, medically oriented EMBASE database, also known as Excerpta Medica. The subset covers medical psychology and psychiatry, addictions, psychoactive drugs, and other psychiatric topics. The EMBASE collection of CDs also includes products in a few other areas that may be of interest to psychology students and researchers, such as neuroscience and pharmacy.

FAMLYSCI
Send e-mail to
LISTSERV@LSV.UKY.EDU
Put in the body of the message:
SUBSCRIBE FAMLYSCI Yourname

The active family science list is a discussion forum for researchers and practitioners in the area of family therapy,

sociology, and psychology. The group is sponsored by the Department of Family Studies at the University of Kentucky.

Indiana University of Pennsylvania Software Collection
anonymous ftp to
ftp.iupui.edu
in the /pub/psychiatry directory

This ftp site contains an older collection of shareware and freeware relevant to mental health professionals such as the ones listed. All zip files are binary, and file names are case sensitive. Some examples follow:

bprs.zip (brief psychiatric rating scale)
communic.zip (evaluates couples' communication patterns)

psycal.zip, psycal1.zip, psycal2.zip, psycal3.zip, psycal4.zip, and psycal5.zip (computer-assisted learning packages for psychiatry)
smokers.zip (helps people stop smoking)
swartz.zip (calculates total lithium level)

C.G. Jung, Analytical Psychology, and Culture
http://www.cgjung.com

The site, founded by Jungian analyst Donald Williams, contains considerable depth for those interested in the work of Carl Jung, including full-text articles and speeches by practicing Jungian analysts, lists of conferences and programs, a guest book, and many relevant links.

Carl Gustav Jung
http://www.enteract.com/~jwalz/Jung

The site is a one-stop reference guide to Jungian concepts and terms. It is presented as a table with "clickable" concepts such as the anima, individuation, and the shadow. One click leads to an entire page about that concept. Also included is a link to the Keirsey Temperament Sorter and one to what Williams calls the Page of Dreams, which contains links to a huge volume of dream-related sites on the Internet.

JungWeb
http://www.onlinepsych.com/jungweb/

This section of the Online Psych Web site is dedicated to Jungian psychology, and it includes information about conferences, institutes, newsgroups, publications, as well as a number of full-text original articles, such as "The Mythical Dimension of Trees" by Herbert W. Schroeder of the USDA Forest Service.

Maslow Publications
http://www.maslow.com/index.html

The Maslow Publications site is a guide for finding materials by Abraham Maslow, who is well known for his theories of motivation and his emphasis on self-actualization. The site lists books in print and books out of print, as well as referenced article listings and information on audiovisual materials.

Mental Health Licensure Resources
http://www.tarleton.edu/~counseling/coresour/lllpc.htm

The Student Counseling Center at Tarleton State University keeps a current record of licensure requirements for the following professions: psychologists, marriage and family therapists, social workers and professional counselors. Requirements are grouped by U.S. federal, state, and current issues. There are also links to exam preparation information.

Mental Health Net
http://www.cmhc.com/

The enormous and very valuable site was designed by frequent Net contributor John Grohol, and it is divided into four main sections: Disorders & Treatments, Professional Resources, Reading Room, and Managed Care & Administration. Its goal is to list every available resource for each mental health topic, including other Web sites, mailing lists, newsgroups, chat rooms, and some of the commercial services. The site offers the full text of *Self-Help Sourcebook Online*, a book containing contact information for self-help groups, an online magazine on mental health issues, several Web-based discussion groups, a yellow pages for clinicians, a job database listing openings in mental health areas, and a huge assortment of links to related sites. It also includes a list of "cyber therapy" sites and a credential check for mental health professionals.

Mind Tools

Mind Tools Ltd.
30 Tanyard Close
Horsham, West Sussex
United Kingdom, RH13 5BN

In the UK:
http://www.mindtools.com/

In the U.S.:
http://www.psych-web/mtsite/
Mind Tools Ltd. in the United Kingdom offers this Web site featuring its software products and a variety of information resources for stress management, time management, problem-solving skills, and other areas of personal growth. Life Plan is one example of its software offerings; it is a program designed to help people clarify their objectives and set daily goals to achieve them. Online brochures on subjects such as brainstorming, critical path analysis, and time management are also available.

National Association of School Psychologists

http://www.naspweb.org/
This site is not only for practicing school psychologists but for parents and teachers as well. The home page features several main sections with names such as "The Family Room" and "The Kitchen," but a Quick Index sidebar offers links to many more resources such as scholarship information, regional news, and ethical issues.

As a public service, NASP sponsors The National Mental Health and Education Center for Children and Families, which is linked to the NASP site. The center is a clearinghouse of information to support families, featuring a wide range of issues from school violence to grade repetition to legislative news.

National Health Information Center

http://nhic-nt.health.org/
This site contains a database of organizations searchable by keyword. The goal is to put consumers in touch with the right organization based on the questions they have.

National Institutes of Health

http://www.nih.gov/

National Institute of Mental Health

http://www.nimh.nih.gov/

NIH and NIMH Web and gopher sites are loaded with information about research, resources, grant programs, and legislative activities.

NPAD News

http://www.npadnews.com
This site features selected articles and resources from the printed version of the *National Panic/Anxiety Disorder Newsletter*, available through subscription. Relevant book reviews, a back issue index, and links to other related sites are also provided. Unfortunately, grant funding has been terminated, so the newsletter and Web site will be discontinued in the near future.

Online Dictionary of Mental Health

http://www.shef.ac.uk/~psysc/psychotherapy/
Sponsored by The Centre for Psychotherapeutic Studies at the Medical School of the University of Sheffield in the UK, the Online Dictionary of Mental

Health is less a dictionary and more a list of links to mental health resources on the Web. The resource is part of the InterPsych Web site, and the resources within it can be accessed alphabetically or by subject.

Online Psych
http://www.onlinepsych.com/

The site is one of the larger online communities with a wide range of resources for those interested in mental health information and support. You can search for books of interest related to various psychological topics, including aging, addiction, parenting, and grief and purchase them online through their secure server. The site includes articles on these topics, as well as a variety of "mindgames," which are primarily self-tests with titles such as "How Jealous Are You?" "Just How Good ARE Your Communication Skills," "The Online IQ Test," and "Are You Close to Burnout?" The site also offers a "treatment locator" so visitors can find mental health professionals in their geographic area.

OUTCMTEN
Send e-mail to
LISTSERV@MAELSTROM.STJOHNS.EDU
Put in the body of the message:
SUBSCRIBE OUTCMTEN Yourname

This mailing list is devoted to mental health outcome evaluations and focuses on problems of assessing and analyzing outcomes of interventions. It is affiliated with the Human Services Research Institute Evaluation Center in Cambridge, Massachusetts, and provides a forum for discussion among mental health stakeholders to improve measurement and assessment strategies.

The Papers of Charles T. Tart
ftp://ftp.ucdavis.edu/pub/fztart/

This ftp site at University of California at Davis contains many of the papers of Charles T. Tart, professor of psychology, who specializes in transpersonal psychology and parapsychology. They deal with a broad range of topics, most of which involve transpersonal psychology. One published paper was called "Multiple Personality, Altered States and Virtual Reality: The World Simulation Process Approach." The papers were either published in print form in journals and reprinted by permission or presented by the author at conferences.

PIT-D
Send e-mail to
LISTSERV@MAELSTROM.STJOHNS.EDU
Put in the body of the message:
SUBSCRIBE PIT-D Yourname

PIT-D is an unmoderated discussion directed to psychotherapists in training. It provides a forum for discussions of training opportunities, theory, research, and supervisory relationships. The list owner (Warren Bush) suggests that the discussion be used as a means of support to help people learning psychotherapy help one another. He discourages supervisors of psychotherapy trainees from participating to maintain a safer environment for free discussion among trainees. Volume is relatively low.

Practice of Psychotherapy
sci.psychology.psychotherapy

This unmoderated newsgroup deals with theoretical and practical issues in psychotherapy and includes psychotherapists and clients. It is active and can occasionally become highly charged. Debates flare about the value of psychotherapy and the use (and abuse) of treatment approaches. After one particularly vitriolic thread was started by an individual, several participants announced their departure from the group. It demonstrates that unmoderated discussion groups are highly dependent on the cooperation, thoughtfulness, and netiquette of the participants.

Prevline
http://www.health.org/

The National Clearinghouse for Alcohol and Drug Information maintains this extensive Web site containing referrals for those with abuse problems, publications, press releases, summaries of recent research and statistics, discussion forums, and related links. Prevline, which is short for Prevention Online, offers access to some useful databases containing bibliographic information related to substance abuse.

Psych Central: Dr. John Grohol's Mental Health Page
http://www.grohol.com/

John Grohol's site offers useful pointers to USENET newsgroups, mailing lists, and Web sites and includes many FAQs and information resources for mental health professionals and consumers. The pointers are valuable and will help participants decide which group best matches their interest. Under the section called Page One lies a diverse collection of articles and op-ed pieces on topics such as self-help books, Internet addiction, psychotherapy, HMOs, and managed care. The site is oriented toward mental health and includes a suicide helpline, a mental disorder symptom list, and a recommended reading list.

Psychotherapy Finances & Managed Care Strategies
http://www.psyfin.com/

In this era of HMO-dominated mental health care and rapidly changing laws and policies, many practitioners struggle to stay abreast and to find their way through the mazes. This site offers information resources for such practitioners. For example, it identifies "hot" niche markets in mental health care: diabetes, downsizing, hypnotherapy, etc., and offers articles and advice about working within and around the managed care system.

PSY-LANG
Send e-mail to
LISTSERV@MAELSTROM.STJOHNS.EDU
Put in the body of the message:
SUBSCRIBE PSY-LANG Yourname

PSY-LANG is a mailing list devoted to the topic of language and psychopathology. It covers subjects such as theories of language and speech, psychopathological speech phenomena, research methods, and ethical issues. Other postings present research papers, reviews of new publications, journal articles, and conferences. With about 400 members from around the world, the list's activity waxes and wanes with short periods of intense discussion followed by long periods of quiet.

PSY-MEDIA
Send e-mail to LISTSERV@LISTS.APA.ORG
Put in the body of the message:
SUBSCRIBE PSY-MEDIA

Formerly called MENTAL-HEALTH-IN-THE-MEDIA, this discussion group moved to a new server with a new list name. The discussion centers on the representation of mental health issues and practitioners in the popular media. Les Posen, the coordinator of this group, promises minimal intervention and encourages participants to broaden their thinking about the conventional concepts of "media" and to discuss electronic media such as film, video, TV, Internet, and CD-ROMs, in addition to the popular press. An interesting discussion dealt with the issue of marketing on the Web by practitioners.

Trials and Tribulations of a Mailing List Owner

As a participant, you may think it's easy to start and maintain a mailing list. Perhaps you think that the owner merely reads the mail, solves an occasional technical glitch, and warns the rare flamer to read the netiquette guidelines. However, Eugenie Georgaca, list owner of PSY-LANG, has had more than her share of problems with the forum devoted to language and psychopathology – some technical and some political. She started out as participant in a general psychiatry mailing list but then, believing the subject matter too broad, asked the list owner if specialized sublists could be supported. Her PSY-LANG sublist was created, along with many others and an organization to manage and support them called InterPsych. However, heated organizational debates, dismissal of the executive director, and a slew of technical problems led the list owners to move to a different server and finally to rethink the entire InterPsych approach. Instead of trying to manage all the lists from a single server, the owners decided to split up and move their individual forums to servers of their choice. The group is now a loose network of discussion groups on specialized issues related to psychology and psychiatry, united administratively and in terms of their common aims.

PSY-LANG participants may have barely noticed all the turbulence underlying their forum as it jumped from server to server. Eugenie, at the Manchester Metropolitan University in the United Kingdom, is pleased that the list serves the members' interests and plans to keep it running for them as smoothly as possible – despite the problems.

PsySpy!
http://idealist.com/cgi-bin/hts-v2.99?psyspy.hts

The PsySpy! Metasearch Tool was developed by Linda Chapman, MSW, to search across various psychology-related databases, several of which she maintains. Database titles include The Wounded Healer Journal, The Child Abuse Yellow Pages, The Child Development Web Site, and Who's Who in Mental Health.

She invites links to other relevant databases as well.

SEXTALK
Send e-mail to
LISTSERV@TAMVM1.TAMU.EDU
Put in the body of the message:
SUBSCRIBE SEXTALK Yourname

SEXTALK is intended to provide a platform for established researchers, clinicians, educators, and students in the field to discuss issues associated with sexuality. Its focus is academic and professional, and, although it is basically open, subscription is not automatic until you have read through the material describing the group's purpose and contact the list owner again to express interest. This may take a few days.

Therapeutic Learning Program
Interactive Health Systems
1337 Ocean Ave., Suite C
Santa Monica, CA 90401
(310) 656-1804
http://www.masteringstress.com

The Therapeutic Learning Program was developed by Roger Gould, an associate clinical professor of psychiatry at UCLA. It helps people sort through their problems by guided menus and assists them with the development of an action plan. The program is designed to be used in consultation with a therapist.

Trauma Info Pages
http://www.trauma-pages.com

David Baldwin, a practicing clinical psychologist and adjunct professor in Oregon, developed a site that offers extensive information about emotional and traumatic stress, including post-traumatic stress disorder (PSTD). The emphasis is on clinical and research issues, such as the psychotherapeutic techniques, outcome studies of trauma survivors, and biological underpinnings. One section includes brochures and handouts on disasters as well as links to related information. The site's Web pages are also offered in Spanish through the automated translation software called Systran.

TURBO_PSY
John C. Pappas
turbopsy@aol.com
http://members.aol.com/turbopsy/
turbopsy.htm

This shareware product is a psychological report writer that allows school psychologists to enter information about a student who has been referred for various reasons. The user enters biographic data, referral information, and test scores and chooses various recommendations from a checklist. An ASCII file is generated that can be converted to word-processing format for editing or expansion. The report itself does more than just repeat the information that was entered. It rephrases the recommendations into full sentences, allows the user to enter extensive text, and provides some feedback on the meaning of common standardized test scores. Registration is $149.

Virtual Reality Exposure (VRE) Therapy
http://www.cc.gatech.edu/gvu/virtual/
Phobia/

In traditional exposure therapy, patients are asked to visualize anxiety-provoking images or situations or they are exposed *in vivo* – to real situations. An inexpensive yet highly effective alternative to these treatments is now possible, thanks to virtual reality. This is not simply a matter of exposing patients to images on a computer screen but, rather, immersing the patient in a virtual situation with a head-mounted display.

This site, sponsored by the VRE team at Georgia Tech, shows examples of VR images used for acrophobia and gives more detail on the advantages of VRE therapy. For example, the procedures can help preserve patient confidentiality by avoiding public places, and they can be finely tuned to meet the exact needs of the patient.

World-Mentalhealth-Networker
Send e-mail to
majordomo@maillist.PEAK.ORG
Put in the body of the message:
SUBSCRIBE world-mentalhealth-networker-list Yourname

Social worker Joan Steinbock is the list owner of World-Mentalhealth-Networker, an open and unmoderated forum for discussing issues of interest to both mental health workers and consumers. The list is fairly new, but Steinbock is making a concerted effort to stimulate discussion by posting intriguing news items and questions.

Software Sources for Practitioners

A number of software products are available to practitioners to help them manage their practices, bill patients, submit insurance forms, provide career

*counseling and guidance, and automate
the process of test administration and
interpretation. Some companies also offer
more comprehensive services and
products, such as workshops and
accessory equipment for biofeedback or
other treatment approaches. Many of the
companies listed have demos but some do
charge for them, so be sure to ask.
Testing materials can usually be ordered
only by licensed psychologists or other
credentialed professionals.*

American Guidance Service (AGS)
4201 Woodland Road
PO Box 99
Circle Pines, MN 55014-1796
(800) 328-2560
http://www.agsnet.com/

Applied Computing Services
2764 Allen Road West
Elk, WA 99009
(800) 553-4055
http://www.pma2000.com
    Applied Computing Services offers
the Client Billing System (CBS) for DOS
platforms, which is practice management
software that integrates with Quicken.

Automated Assessment Associates
PO Box 9447
Salt Lake City, UT 84109
(801) 278-4016
    This company offers SCORES-IT-
ALL, a program that allows the
psychologist to create an automated
scoring system for a variety of testing
scenarios, as well as interpretive
reporting software.

BHS Publishing
(800) 769-6689
    BHS provides billing and practice
management software for Macintosh or
Windows platforms (MACPsych Billing
Version 3.0).

Blumenthal Software, Inc.
PO Box 138, SVS
Binghamton, NY 13903
(607) 724-0032
jerblum@spectra.net

The company offers patient billing
software featuring open item accounting.

Cambridge Software Labs
45 Highland Road
Boxford, MA 01921
(978) 352-8909
    The company offers "The Cure,"
patient billing software with extra
features such as schedule management
and checkbook balancing. The current
version is available for DOS platforms,
and a Windows version is under
development.

CareerPoint 5.0
Conceptual Systems, Inc.
1010 Wayne Avenue, Suite 1420
Silver Spring, MD 20910
(301) 589-1800
http://www.concepsys.com
    This Windows program by Steve
Forrer and Zandy Leibowitz is a career
development system for organizations
and includes modules on self-
assessment, organizational assessment,
career goals, and career planning.

CFKR
11860 Kemper Road, Unit 7
Auburn, CA 95603
(800) 525-5626
CFKR@CFKR.com
    Specializing in career education
and development materials, the company
offers a catalog containing video, print,
and computer software in areas such as
job skills, vocational preparation, career
assessment, and college planning.

Chronicle Guidance Publications, Inc.
PO Box 1190
Moravia, NY 13118-1190
(800) 622-7284
http://www.chronicleguidance.com
    The company offers a range of
products in the area of career and life
skills development, including a number
of CD-ROMs.

Civerex Systems, Inc.
48 Lakeshore Road, Suite 1
Pointe Claire, Quebec H9S 4H4 Canada
(514) 630-1005

civerex@civerex.com
http://www.civerex.com
    Civerex offers Civer-Psych 2.0 (for Windows 95 or NT), which is a program for practitioners with modules for intake and assessment, diagnosis, treatment planning and billing, within the framework of DSM-IV diagnoses.

CPT Management Systems
2455 Bennet Valley Road
Suite 210-C
Santa Rosa, CA 95404
(800) 477-4907
CPTbil@aol.com
    CPT sells mental health billing (CPT Billing) and office management software, formerly called MacPsych Billing. Their new products run on Macintosh and Windows platforms.

Creative Research Systems, Inc.
140 Vista View #100
Petaluma, CA 94952
(707) 765-1001
http://www.surveysystem.com
    Creative Research offers an automated survey system.

MicroEye
17560 Road 85B
Esparto, CA 95627
(800) 787-3194
http://www.microeye.com
    Psychotherapy Office Planner is the practice management and billing software offered by the company, in Windows or Macintosh formats.

Mindmedia
849 Almar Avenue
Suite C-125-C
Santa Cruz, CA 95060
(800) 818-9445
http://www.mindmedia.com/
    Mindmedia offers self-help resources and software.

Nijo Software
(914) 722-9011
seh5@columbia.edu
http://www.travel-net.com/~alphalog/
    Nijo offers software for IBM-compatible computers to automate the administration of the Personality Diagnostic Questionnaire (PDQ-4).

Outer Montana Systems
PO Box 661
Nevada City, CA 95959
(530) 265-5612
(800) 588-6824
http://www.omsweb.com
    The company offers a Windows-based patient billing software package called Touched in full, billing-only, and "super lite" versions for group or solo practices.

J & J Engineering
22797 Holgar Ct., NE
Poulsbo, WA 98370
(888) 550-8300
http://www.jjengineering.com
    Physiodata offers software and equipment to support practitioners using biofeedback in their practice.

Psychological Assessment Resources, Inc. (PAR)
PO Box 998
Odessa, FL 33556
(813) 968-3003
(800) 331-TEST
http://www.parinc.com
    PAR distributes books, testing materials, software, and other resources used by professional psychologists. A variety of computer-based psychological testing programs are available.

Psychologistics, Inc.
PO Box 033896
Indialantic, FL 32903
(407) 259-7811
http://www.crw-sys.com
    The company offers several software programs for practicing psychologists, including common assessment and interview instruments, interpretive software, and practice management/billing software (Shrink).

Psychometric Software, Inc.
2210 S. Front St., Suite 208
Melbourne, FL 32901
(800) 882-9811
http://www.digital.net

The company offers a number of software products for IBM-compatible computers to assist practitioners, including computer-based test interpretations of several major psychological tests (MMPI-2, MMPI-A, MCMI-III, Bender Gestalt), practice management software, a program to assess vocational interests, and software that allows you to develop your own test administration and scoring programs.

Psychotherapy Practice Manager
J. H. Mullin, Ph.D.
113 Hueneme Avenue
Channel Islands, CA 93035
(800) 895-1618
http://www.anacapa.net/~jhmullin
The company offers practice management software (Windows and Mac) called TPPM for clinical records, billing, and appointments.

ROR-SCAN
9297 Siempre Viva Road, Suite 71-169
San Diego, CA 92173
(702) 598-1209
rorscan@laguna.com.mx
The ROR-SCAN programs provide a computer-based approach to the scoring and interpretation of patient responses to Rorschach tests.

Saner Software
37 West 222, Route 64, Suite 253
St. Charles, IL 60175
(800) 448-9071
Saner offers ShrinkRapt, a billing and insurance program for Windows or Mac computers.

Shrink2Fit Software
215 North Cayuga Street
Suite 103
Ithaca, NY 14850
(607) 273-9169
(800) 440-3859
Shrink2Fit advertises Solo, practice management software for the Macintosh.

Psych Solutions
41 William Fairfield Drive
Wenham, MA 01984

(978) 468-2290
http://www.psychsolutions.com
PsychOffice for the Macintosh is practice management software that includes billing, correspondence, patient records, and scheduling. The company also offers an automated quality assessment and reporting system.

Stens Corporation
6451 Oakwood Drive
Oakland, CA 94611-1350
(800) 257-8367
http://www.stens-biofeedback.com
Stens distributes a variety of biofeedback instrumentation products and software, some of which can be used with microcomputers.

SumTime Software
3748 North Causeway Boulevard
Suite 300
Metairie, LA 70002
(504) 828-2551
(800) 767-5788
http://www.sumtime.com
SumTime provides practice management/billing software for psychotherapists, for Windows or Macintosh platforms. An electronic claims kit that links to a claims clearinghouse is available as an add-on.

Synergistic Office Solutions, Inc.
17445 East Apshawa Road
Clermont, FL 34711-9049
(352) 242-9100
http://www.sosoft.com
Practice, office, and case management software is offered for Windows machines.

Western Psychological Services
12031 Wilshire Blvd.
Los Angeles, CA 90025-1251
(310) 478-2061
The company distributes computerized psychological testing and scoring materials.

Abuse Survivors' Resources
http://www.tezcat.com/~tina/psych.shtml
A site devoted to resources for victims of abuse, this page offers links to discussion groups, FAQs, organizations, and descriptions of various patterns of abuse and their effects.

Adoptees' Mailing List Home Page
http://psy.ucsd.edu/~jhartung/adoptees.html
Jeff Hartung, administrator of the adoptees' mailing list, provides extensive links to legal information and legislation concerning the rights of adopted children, birth parents, and adoptive parents, plus many adoption-related links.

Al-Anon and Alateen
http://www.Al-Anon-Alateen.org
Al-Anon and Alateen sponsor this Web site as a supplement to their self-help recovery programs for families and friends of alcoholics. The site offers access to a directory of Al-Anon regional offices and services and other contact points. Material on this site can be displayed in a number of different langauges, an appropriate feature for this worldwide organization.

alt.support._____
The alt.support series of newsgroups and a few related cousins also in the alt category provide forums for an enormous range of psychology-related disorders. The topics cover a broad spectrum, such as anxiety-panic disorders, depression, sleep disorders, Tourette's syndrome, schizophrenia, and attention deficit disorder. These groups

offer an online outlet to discuss experiences in a relatively anonymous environment, and many participants become permanent contributors who rely heavily on the support they receive. They also gain satisfaction by offering help to others with similar problems. The nature of the group discussions varies widely, partly depending on the current thread and the people participating. Some groups are more supportive than others, and you'll need armored skin for a few of them. Conversation can sometimes become acerbic, hostile, or tasteless, but for the most part, much of what happens in these groups appears to provide real support and information sharing for their participants.

Ask the Expert: Kim Martyn
http://www.sexscape.org/askkim/
This service is part of the Web site called SexScape.Org. Kim Martyn, a health educator, answers the "sex question of the week," chosen from the questions submitted. Subjects include circumcision, lost desire for sex, strange fantasies, rape counseling, and oral sex. Martyn's answers are usually thoughtful and tactful.

Autism Resources
http://web.syr.edu/~jmwobus/autism/
The site offers information and resources for people concerned about autism, especially parents with an autistic child. Links to programs that offer treatment for autism are included, as well as accounts of people who have personal experiences with the disorder.

Bootstraps
http://www.selfhelp.com/bootstraps.html
Sponsored by Three Waters Press and created by Keith Ellis, the Bootstraps Web site offers a monthly column devoted to self-help and self-I

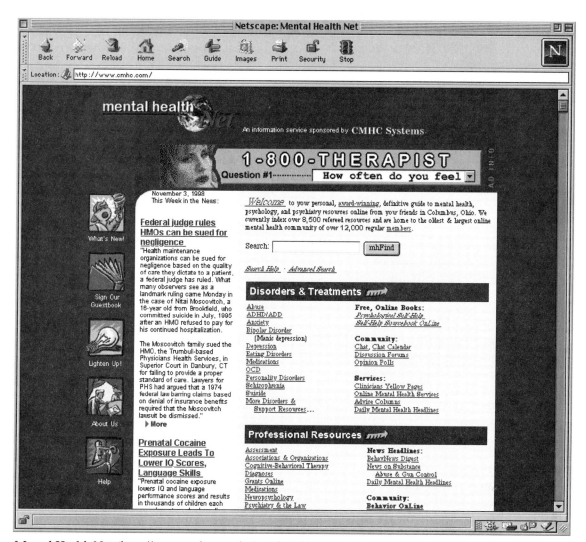

Mental Health Net (http://www.cmhc.com/). Reprinted by permission.

mprovement. The columns are usually in a question-and- answer format, and visitors can send in their own questions. Ellis is the author of *The Magic Lamp, How to Make Certain Your Wishes Come True.*

Calendar of Mental Health Chats
http://www.cmhc.com/chatcal.htm

Mental Health Net includes this searchable calendar of live chats which take place on various Web sites and chat servers throughout the world. The entries in the calendar focus on chats about depression, anxiety/panic, eating disorders, and related mental health topics.

CH.A.D.D. (Children and Adults with Attention Deficit Disorders)
http://www.chadd.org/

The Web page of the nonprofit, parent-based organization called Children and Adults with Attention Deficit Disorders offers advice to parents on treatments, summaries of media coverage of the disorder, a bibliography of books and publications, conference information, and a full list of regional CH.A.D.D. chapters in several countries.

Cocaine Anonymous Home Page
http://www.ca.org/

This site offers information and resources for people who want to escape from cocaine addiction. Cocaine Anonymous is the support group that sponsors it. The page includes a self-test for addiction.

CYBERSHRINK
http://www.cybershrink.com

Sheree Motto and Michael Adamse, two practicing clinical psychologists, used this site to collect information from the Web-surfing audience for a book on the psychology of Internet relationships entitled *Online Friendship, Chat-Room Romance and Cybersex.* Their Web site promotes the book with excerpts, reviews, and a request for further contributions for future projects.

Depression Resources List
http://earth.execpc.com/~corbeau/

The page, compiled by Dennis Taylor, includes links to a variety of resources for people who suffer from depression or who are researching the disorder. Descriptions of the disorder, current research, and even poetry and prose from sufferers are included in this compendium.

False Memory Syndrome
http://fmsf.com

Linda Chapman, MSW, has produced a comprehensive site about "false memory syndrome," featuring many full-text journal articles, resources for survivors, and legal references. One such reference is a link to *The Repressed Memory Psych/Law Newsletter,* "a monthly publication that provides a comprehensive, practical, and informational outlet for lawyers and for psychology professionals who provide plaintiff expert witness services in sexual abuse cases."

Chapman thoughtfully includes a section on comic relief, with a link to the "False Malady Sympathy Foundation."

Habit Smart
http://www.cts.com/crash/habtsmrt/

The site is dedicated to providing information about the latest research in the area of addictive behavior and treatment. It provides a newsletter called "The Archivist," which summarizes research studies, access to articles in back issues of the newsletter, a self-scoring alcohol check-up questionnaire, and links to other addiction-related sites.

Internet Mental Health Home Page
http://www.mentalhealth.com/

Brian Chow and Phillip W. Long of Vancouver, Canada, developed this free encyclopedia of mental health information for the public. It includes considerable information about disorders and medications, as well as a magazine section with book reviews, brochures, and a selection of full-text articles on mental health issues from sources such as the *Medical Post, Scientific American,* the *Harvard Mental Health Letter,* and *MacLean's.*

Therapy Online

Psychologists offer therapy in many different formats, and online delivery has grown substantially. The relative anonymity of cyberspace may be a key reason. People are often more willing to self-disclose in this kind of environment, compared with a face-to-face setting. Prices for a single "session," which is usually a response to an e-mail query describing the problem, start around $20. Below is a service that helps in choosing an online therapist:

Metanoia Guide to Internet Mental Health Services
http://www.metanoia.org/imhs/
With the advent of psychological help being delivered online, it seems almost necessary that a site like the Metanoia Guide (metanoia is Greek for "a change of mind") exist not only to rate providers but to check their credentials as well. The Metanoia Guide includes detailed information about topics such as confidentiality, ethics, and, of course, payment methods. Its provider directory is divided into those giving single answers, those giving ongoing support, and uncredentialed providers. A typical listing gives pricing information, rating (0-4 stars), and communication information (e-mail, phone, chat, etc.). This service is co-sponsored by Mental Health Net.

CyberSayer

http://cybersayer.com/

CyberSayer software for Windows (US$55) is a self-help program designed to provide insights and clarity for life planning and business decisions. One component, called "The Eye of Horus," is a database of insights relevant to various situations in life with options to receive feedback regarding your own life path, finances, friendships, business interests, and other areas. The site also includes a vivid graphics section on what your eyes tell you about yourself. It categorizes personalities into different eye types, depending on whether the eyes have color flecks, jewels, or other characteristics. There is no research basis for these categories, but the site is colorful.

tAPir (The Anxiety-Panic Internet Resource)

http://www.algy.com/anxiety/

The site provides resources dealing with panic and anxiety disorders, including descriptions of the disorders, lists of support groups, treatment approaches, stories from sufferers, medications, and bibliographies.

Pendulum Resources

http://www.pendulum.org

The site supplements the Pendulum mailing list, a support group dealing with bipolar affective disorder, more commonly known as manic-depression. It offers resources to help you identify whether you are suffering from this disorder, research reports and summaries, links to legal sites that provide information on the rights of someone diagnosed with disorders of this kind, and lists of relevant conferences and contact points.

Practice of Psychotherapy

sci.psychology.psychotherapy

The unmoderated newsgroup discusses psychotherapy, drug

treatments, ethical issues, and other topics, primarily among people who have experienced psychotherapy themselves. Acidic debates break out, particularly over the value of psychotherapy. Many cross-postings to other psychology-related newsgroups are included.

Self-Help & Psychology
http://www.well.com/user/selfhelp/

The Web site, sponsored by *Self-Help & Psychology Magazine*, contains reviews, articles, a professional corner, links to other sites, a bookshelf area, and other features. In the articles section, the site is divided into departments with diverse titles such as Loss & Bereavement, Alcohol/Nicotine/Drugs, Men, Work & Career, Depression & Anxiety, Aging, Sexuality, and CyberRomance. Within the departments are FAQs, current research summaries, brochures and short articles by experts in the field, bibliographies, and links to other online resources. The site solicits donations and offers free subscriptions to a self-help e-mail newsletter.

SEX-L
**Send e-mail to
LISTSERV@TAMVM1.TAMU.EDU
Put in the body of the message:
SUBSCRIBE SEX-L Yourname**

This extremely high-volume list is an open discussion of sexuality and relationships. Some things are off limits, such as flaming, harassment, graphics files, attachments, and direct requests for intercourse, but almost nothing else is. Due to the high volume, the list owner gives stringent directions about subject lines and the inclusion of text from previous messages. If you subscribe, you may want to send another message to the LISTSERV address that has SET SEX-L DIGEST in the body of the message to

avoid a constant barrage in your e-mail box.

Voices of Adoption
http://www.ibar.com/voices

The site contains personal essays by adoptees and birthparents as well as links to adoption-related events, chat rooms, articles, literature, and resources for learning how to become active in adoption issues.

Web of Addictions
http://www.well.com/user/woa/

The purpose of this site is to disseminate accurate information about alcohol and other drug addictions. It provides FAQs, treatment information, links to net resources on addictions, and a "Rolodex" of contact points.

Walkers in Darkness
http://www.walkers.org
Subscribe to mailing list via Web site.

The Web site and mailing list form a complementary set of resources for people suffering from depression. The Web site offers links to related sites, FAQs about depression, photographs of people participating in Walkers events, drug information, and pointers to other newsgroups. On the mailing list, people discuss their experiences and seek support from fellow participants. Walkers in Darkness resources are widely known and well respected as an excellent source of support.

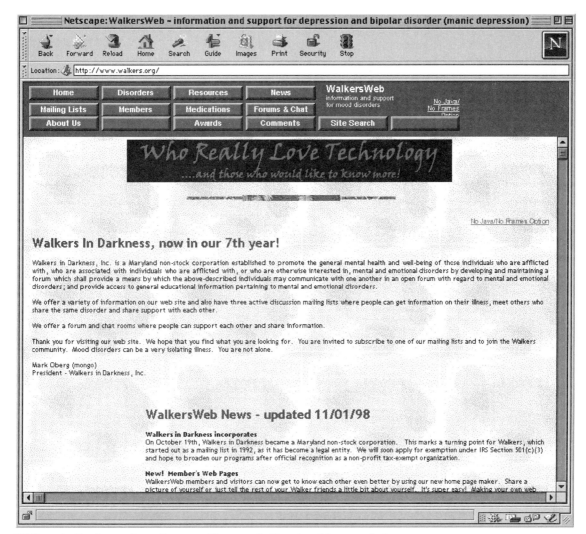

Walkers in Darkness (http://www.walkers.org/). Reprinted by permission.

Wing of Madness: A Depression Guide

http://members.aol.com/depress/index.htm

This page is written by Deb Deren, who suffers from the disorder, in the interest of educating others about depression. It includes a layperson's description of the disorder, her experiences with it, and a brief screening test for depression, along with links to other resources.

Index